ACT
NORMAL

Moving Compassion from Niche to Norm

D0067109

Scott Wilson
With Patrick Springle

I'd like to dedicate this book to my grandmother, Frances Wilson. She is 102 years old and still serving the Lord with all her heart. She released her first book on her 100th birthday. It's entitled, **My First 100 Years**. She still leads a small group Bible Study each week and reads the Bible every day. She beats me at dominoes every time we play (she won't let me keep score which makes me think she cheats). I want to be like my Granny when I grow up.

SPECIAL MESSAGE FROM DR. WOOD

Dear Leader,

Let me be the first to introduce to you Influence. Leaders are influencers. You are surrounded by people you influence every day, and you are influenced by others. Today is the beginning of something new. Influence is more than a conference; it's a leadership resource provider. The resources produced by church leaders in partnership with Influence are practical, relevant and proven. They are written by your peers who are working alongside you in ministry every day.

The book you hold in your hand—Act Normal by Scott Wilson, Senior Pastor of The Oaks Fellowship in Red Oak, TX—is just the first resource of many already being produced under the Influence label.

Act Normal is a campaign designed for churches to motivate those merely involved to move to God's standard of normal, spirit led, compassionate, and generous lives modeled in the book of Acts. The book is just the first component of this campaign. Other resources will follow such as a DVD series, small group curriculum and journal.

Future resources are already in the works and will be released in the near future. Influence isn't established in a moment; it's the culmination of many moments. It's not about one day; it's about every day. The resources you will see coming from Influence in the coming months will help develop, strengthen, and improve your leadership and your everyday ministry, and expand your ability to influence your community for Jesus Christ.

Welcome to Influence!

George O. Wood
General Superintendent, The General Council of the Assemblies of God

Contents

ACKNOWLEDGEMENTS

I want to say a big thank you to all the people of The Oaks Fellowship. I love you so much. Thank you for letting me be your pastor. I greatly appreciate the staff and the elders of The Oaks who have encouraged me every step of the way in the process of writing this book.

I'd also like to thank my brothers Brent, Bracy, and Dallas, for helping me remember so many of the stories that I've included in this book. I love you guys.

I'm thankful for my teaching team and the staff who put so much time into this book-Paul Hurckman, Chris Railey, John Davidson, and Emily Van Wie. You guys are awesome. Also, a huge thanks to Justin Lathrop, Andrea Lathrop, and Steve Blount for all you've done to get this book and the ACT NORMAL campaign to as many churches, communities, and people as possible. Thousands of people are going to be touched because of your efforts.

I'd like to recognize my friend and writer, Pat Springle, who has truly been a gift from God to me. I respect and appreciate you so very much. You are not only a gifted communicator, but also a man of great character and strength. Thank you for all your contribution and diligent work on this book.

Finally, I would like to thank my wife Jenni and our three boys—Dillon, Hunter, and Dakota. I'm so proud of you. Thank you for being such a wonderful family and for letting me share your stories in yet another book. I love you.

FOREWORD

I've never been a big fan of a normal life.

I was my parents' last shot at having a son. As my mother's 13th pregnancy, I followed ten miscarriages. I had a speech problem, so I grew up going to resource class (where they put us kids who were a little more creative in the pace of our learning). I'm fully Italian -- in case my name didn't give that away. When I was younger I lived to surf. Then a guy carrying a cross down the beach gave me a tract, and a few days later I got saved. Several months after that, I went to Bible College, and a few years later my young wife and I planted a church. I was 28 and she was 23. And now–almost 18 years later–we're still pastoring that church.

Not much normal about that! But then again, maybe normal isn't what we think. Maybe, as followers of Jesus, we need to rethink normal. It's not that we want to stick out like sore thumbs on humanity, but that we are created to stand out because we are crafted to fit into God's definition of normal.

That's exactly what I see in Scott Wilson's book and in his life. He lives according to a different normal than most.

The book of Acts is our best view into what God had in mind when He launched the first church plants ever. It was people who were Jesus freaks, filled with the Holy Spirit, going throughout the world doing things we consider amazing and exceptional for the Kingdom.

But maybe–just maybe–they were doing exactly what God considers normal for His people. They preached the Gospel, and many followed. They stood up when the pressure was tense. They served widows. They cared for the poor. They had compassion for the hurting.

The book of Acts is the normal that we as today's Church need to reset our expectation meters to.

As you read this book, it is my prayer that your eyes will be opened to things you never saw before in the book of Acts... things God wants you to consider normal that you previously thought to be outrageous and beyond His expectations of you... things that you cannot do on your own as a normal person, but as a normal follower of Jesus Christ are simply what you live to do.

And personally, I believe that one of the greatest of these things is having a heart of compassion for the poor, the lost, the forgotten, and those who are hurting. That's the crowd Jesus tended to be found among.

This is one principle I've found to be true: If you want to be where Jesus loves to be, start serving the poor. If you want to see Jesus, look into the eyes of an orphan in Swaziland, Africa. You can find him in the eyes of a girl who is trapped by human trafficking in Thailand. And you can find him in the eyes of a homeless man under the interstate overpass in Baton Rouge, and in the eyes of a single mom in San Diego struggling to pay her bills.

Jesus is here. All around us. We just need to let Him open our eyes so that we can see. And then... only then... can we truly act normal.

Jesus is here. Anything can happen.

Dino Rizzo

Lead Pastor

Healing Place Church

http://dinorizzo.com

http://twitter.com/dinorizzo

INTRODUCTION
WHAT'S NORMAL, ANYWAY?

What is "the normal Christian life"? If we put the names of all Christians across the globe into a hat, and selected a dozen or so to observe for a few weeks, what could we conclude is a "normal" life for people who claim to know Christ? Undoubtedly, we would notice that some of them are full of passion and joy. They live their lives like they're on a mission. And they are! Their lives overflow with words of kindness and acts of compassion toward others. When faced with difficult circumstances or challenges, they pray, read Scripture, and trust God to lead them into right decisions. They're not content to just slide through life or simply get by, but are determined to make a difference. Something powerfully moves them to be more, want more, and do more.

Sadly, however, we would also observe others who seem to be simply going through the motions of life—attending church a few times, singing songs about God, putting a few dollars in the offering plate, and maybe showing up for a Bible study now and again. Though they appear to be religious, in reality, their daily lives are not much different from countless others who don't know God at all.

Which one, then, is normal?

Luke's Audience

When Luke penned his history of the early church, he wanted to give Theophilus, who may have been a Roman governor and possibly sponsored Luke's efforts to write, a true and accurate account of the events that transpired. In his writings, however, Luke does not start with the events of the early church. His first history book focused on the life of Jesus, again for his friend Theophilus. We know these books of the New Testament, Luke and Acts, as two separate documents removed from one another by the insertion of John's gospel. It is important to know that the early readers of Luke's writings may have had both documents combined into a single history lesson: Luke-Acts. The reason this is important is because readers today need to understand that Luke's account of the early church, the Book of Acts, is an extension of the work of Christ, the Book of Luke, and should not be viewed as a completely separate era. Before Jesus ascended to heaven, he gave the people on the hillside a strange message: "I'm leaving, the Holy Spirit will be with you to lead and empower you, but I'll be with you until the end of the age." Was Jesus leaving or not? Would he be absent from his followers, or would he remain present? Actually, it was the best of both worlds. Jesus would still be as close as their breath, but he would live in them through the power of the Spirit of God. His authority, love, and strength would be theirs in a different, more all-encompassing way than they had known—even when he was walking with them on the dusty streets and roads of Palestine.

Do we understand this promise? The presence and power of Jesus would be fully available to anyone who trusted in Jesus, not just to the ones who looked up into the sky as he vanished that day, but to every believer from that day until his return. When we look at Luke's history of the early church, we're amazed at how God worked in and through the believers of that day, but should we be surprised? When we hear the testimony of someone today who has seen God work in a wonderful way, we ooh and ahh at the magnificence of the Spirit's tenderness and power, but should we be shocked? We shouldn't be surprised when the Almighty God chooses to reveal his power and grace through Spirit-filled, Spirit-led, Spirit-empowered people who are sold out to his cause. I'm not talking about cardboard cutout Christians who claim to have no problems and a life that is always sunny. No, I'm talking about real people who live in the real world with deep hurts and high hopes—people like you and me.

We sometimes glorify the believers of the early church and put them up on a pedestal as super Christians, but that's a complete misunderstanding of who these people were. The ones who "turned the world upside down" in those first years after Christ returned to heaven would not have been on any corporate headhunter's list of top prospects. They were blue-collar men and women with little education. They were people who experienced challenges, fear, and doubts. (Did I mention they were like you and me?) But they had one crucial attribute: they were open to the Spirit of God. They said to God, "I'm not much, but I'm all yours. Do with me whatever you want."

In both of Luke's histories, he makes the point over and over that Jesus reversed the standards of his day; outsiders (prostitutes, tax gatherers, women, foreigners, lepers, blind people, etc.) became insiders in God's kingdom, and the supposed insiders (Pharisees, Sadducees, and Scribes) became outsiders because they resisted God's grace. In addition, when we look at the people who made up the early church, we are mistaken if we wish our church could be a "New Testament" church because the churches Paul visited drove him nuts! They engaged in sexual sins, arrogance, idolatry of riches, drunkenness, conflict, bitterness, and every other sin that can be named. Though we may think we don't qualify for the position of "follower of Christ" because we've blown it, have few skills, or have deep, dark secrets in our past, in reality we are prime candidates for his kingdom! Because God delights in people who are humble enough to admit their need for him. The "normal" Christian life is one of humility and repentance, which opens our hearts to experience the depths of God's love, forgiveness, and power.

Some Christians have the faulty concept that if they could just walk with Jesus in the flesh, everything would make sense and life would go well for them. But the disciples didn't change very much until Jesus left the earth and the power of the Holy Spirit invaded their bodies and souls. This is what people need today—the invasion of the Spirit into the nooks and crannies of their lives, to be transformed by grace from the inside out so that they delight in obeying the One who proved his love by dying for all.

The Christian life is immediate, yet at the same time progressive. It begins in a moment, but continues to grow throughout our life, as we continually trust God to direct us. For me, it began when I went on a youth ministry trip to Arkansas. There, God spoke to me through his word. He asked, "Are you going to keep playing games with your faith, or are you ready to give me everything you've got?" In that moment, I knew God was asking me to give him everything I am, everything I possess, and everything I'll ever be. I said, "Yes," and I was excited about what the future held. I didn't want to miss out on anything God had in store for me. Suddenly, I realized I'd been afraid of God. Now, however, my relationship with him was firmly planted in his love and grace. This made all the difference in the world. I now obeyed because I wanted to please him, not because I was terrified of him. From that day on, I've learned what the normal Christian life is all about. Every day, I've tried to surrender myself to Christ's authority and live for his kingdom. Though I have a long way to go, I'm thrilled to be in the center of God's will, basking in the Spirit's love, and filled with his power to accomplish his will. It's a great, but often, bumpy ride!

I've talked to men and women whose lives have been ignited by the flame of God's love. Each one can tell stories of apathy and resistance during different periods of their lives, but they all point to a time when God touched their hearts and assured them of his presence and purpose. Without this life-changing transformation, we can go through all the motions of the Christian faith, but remain empty, sterile, and dry inside. We have to begin with a genuine experience of the grace of God.

The Mission

It's easy to look at the church today and complain that it's not what God intends it to be. But until Jesus returns in glory, we will have to wrestle with the realities of living in this life. This is not a bad thing. The grace of God is revealed when men and women have the courage to admit their sins and thank God for his marvelous forgiveness. The power of God is revealed when people admit their weaknesses and trust God to give them strength to tackle life's most difficult situations. But to experience this grace and power we have to be honest with ourselves and begin where we are. Instead of covering up our pain and sins, we need to find the courage to admit them to God, and perhaps, to another person we can trust.

History, I believe, can be divided into four momentous movements: creation, the fall into sin, redemption through the death and resurrection of Christ, and the ultimate restoration of everything in the New Heaven and Earth. As believers today, we live between the already and the not yet, the grace that has been given to us as "a down payment" and the ultimate reality one day of living in God's presence forever. While we're here, we're not alone. God has not abandoned us and wished us "Good luck!" as we live out our years on this earth. We have been given three realities to help us through this journey: the Spirit of God, the word of God, and the people of God. Throughout this book, we will see how God orchestrated the music of these three beautiful instruments to produce a symphony of grace in the early church—and how he wants to do the same thing in you and me today.

Each day, we'll look at a passage from Acts that will inspire and help us grasp how we can live a normal Christian life as described in the Bible. God's word is living and active. It pierces our hearts, fills us with hope, and directs our steps. God has always used his word to shape the lives of believers. In his book, The Last Word, N. T. Wright observes that in the early church, the word of God was "planted firmly in the soil of the missionary community, confronting the powers of the world with the news of the Kingdom of God, refreshed and invigorated by the Spirit, growing particularly through the preaching and teaching of the apostles, and bearing fruit in the transformation of human lives as the start of God's project to put the whole cosmos to rights." Is that a big enough mission for you and me, to "put the whole cosmos to rights"? That's God's ultimate plan: to restore men and women to himself, to restore his kingdom to earth in some measure today, to overcome evil and redeem the lost, and eventually, to restore all creation and make it better than it was when Adam and Eve lived in the Garden. God's word is central to this effort.

Before You Begin...

Luke depicts the normal Christian life in Acts in all its rich texture and complexity. He describes miracles that demonstrate God's power, but he also records times of waiting, confusion, and seeking God for direction. In one moment, Peter is miraculously rescued, but sadly, James is put to death with a sword. We witness the lives of humble people transformed by grace, and we read accounts of brutal torture and the murder of God's people. Luke doesn't offer his readers a "happy-ever-after" story, but rather, a description of people with genuine faith, devoted to God, and filled with the Spirit who trusts God through thick and thin.

Courage. That's the trait I see as I read through the pages of Acts. In this book, we'll look at 31 other traits that rely on courage to make them real in our lives. These traits are not boxes to check off to prove we are believers. They are descriptions of an individual who loves God and is sold out to him. Don't try to manufacture them. When the Holy Spirit points out areas where you are weak (and I promise he will), respond with humility, admit your need for his grace, trust God to guide and change you, and choose to obey out of gratitude for his mercy.

Before you begin, I want to ask you to consider making two commitments: First, pray and ask God to open your heart to hear from him. Pour out your heart and trust him to fill you with his power and grace. Tell him that you'll go where he wants you to go, and you'll be what he wants you to be. And during these 31 days, listen for his Spirit to affirm your heart's commitment and direct you. If you do that, God will change your life—I promise. My hope is that as you study and pray through this book, your relationship with God will become vibrant, authentic, and life changing. Don't just read the book, finish it, and put it back on the shelf for future reference. Make a commitment to take bold steps to put your faith into action.

Second, become a part of the 50/50 challenge. As an expression of the heart of joyful service Luke describes in Acts, I want to ask you to participate in one of the most exciting adventures a community can experience: a bold strategy for compassionate service. In our church and community, I'm asking 20,000 people to devote 50 hours and $50 over the next year to community service. I want to encourage you to think outside the box for what your church and community can do. Don't just look for ways you can serve and give inside the four walls of your church, but allow God to open your eyes to the thousands of needs in your community. The Spirit of God will help you uncover dozens of opportunities in your community if you'll let him: helping a neighbor move into a house, giving blood, leading a support group, coaching a children's sports team, caring for a foster child, and many others. The list is endless. We'll point you to a wide variety of projects to consider. Some of them will appeal to you, others won't. That's not a problem. Give the $50 to anyone God puts on your heart. In fact, put $50 in a special place in your purse or wallet, and ask God to lead you to give it to a person on the side of the road, a ministry on the other side of the world, or anything in between.

As you consider investing your time and money, trust God for direction and dive in. I'm excited to see the impact this campaign is going to have in our communities as we collectively devote a million hours and a million dollars to touch people's lives in selfless, tangible ways. I think most people who are recipients of this grace will pay it forward to others in need. I'm so excited about the potential for this campaign to change people's lives.

If you're up to the challenge and want to be a part of this community-changing effort, go to www.actnormal.org and register. We want to encourage you throughout this next year by sending you inspirational stories of what people are doing to serve their community and give you ideas of what you can do. We also want to hear your story… so put the book down right now and go to www.actnormal.org and register.

Luke's history of the early church was a continuation of the ministry of Jesus as the Spirit worked in the lives of those he loved. Today, the Spirit of Jesus continues to live in you and me. In the same way the Father sent Jesus into the world, today he sends us, not just to proclaim the good news of forgiveness and new life, but to be living examples of God's Grace so that people will sit up and take notice. It's the greatest adventure the world has ever known. Are you ready to live a normal Christian life?

DAY ONE | WAITING

"On one occasion, while [Jesus] was eating with them, he gave them this command: 'Do not leave Jerusalem, but wait for the gift my Father promised, which you have heard me speak about. For John baptized with water, but in a few days you will be baptized with the Holy Spirit' " (Acts 1:4).

Popular author and pastor Chuck Swindoll has said that waiting is the most difficult task a Christian can perform. I hate to wait, and I suspect I'm not alone. It's fascinating that Jesus instructs his followers to spend an extended time waiting before the gospel is to be brought to the world. How did they respond? We can only surmise that many of them had a difficult time. Interestingly, Paul reports that over 500 people saw Jesus between his resurrection and ascension back to heaven, however in Jerusalem, ten days later, we count only 120 people. The majority of those who had witnessed the most amazing event in history must have said, "No thanks."

When Jesus told them to wait and pray, they did what most of us would do: they asked questions. "Is this it?" they wondered. "Are you going to inaugurate your kingdom and rule on earth when these days of waiting are up?" I can almost see Jesus shake his head and smile like he must have done a thousand times before. He gently corrected and instructed them again. He said, "It is not for you to know the times or dates the Father has set by his own authority. But you will receive power when the Holy Spirit comes on you; and you will be my witnesses in Jerusalem, and in all Judea and Samaria, and to the ends of the earth." (Acts 1:7-8). Despite these words, his followers still thought Jesus was going to stay on earth and rule through a political kingdom, but he had different plans. He was going to leave and put the enterprise in their hands. He gave them a strategy: first, tell people near you; second, expand your reach to neighboring lands; and third, tell everyone on earth.

Before implementing these three steps, however, he told them to wait. I wonder what they were thinking when he lifted off the dirt and disappeared into a cloud. They must have been amazed and afraid at the same time. I would have been shaking my head in confusion, muttering, "Great. There he goes. That's pretty cool, but what are we going to do now?"

The feast of Pentecost was celebrated fifty days after the Sabbath of Passover week, and ten days after the ascension. As the faithful men and women prayed together that day, the promise of the Holy Spirit became a stunning reality. Weeks before, on the night Jesus was arrested, he told the disciples that the Father was going to send the Holy Spirit to them to be their counselor and to lead them into all truth. This moment at Pentecost was the fulfillment of that promise. In the Scriptures, wind is used as a symbol of the Spirit's presence, and fire represents God's holiness. Luke tells us, "Suddenly a sound like the blowing of a violent wind came from heaven and filled the whole house where they were sitting. They saw what seemed to be tongues of fire that separated and came to rest on each of them. All of them were filled with the Holy Spirit and began to speak in other tongues as the Spirit enabled them" (Acts 2:2-4).

This was no "barely visible" manifestation of God; it wasn't something a single person imagined. This was a cataclysmic event. The sound of the wind was like a tornado or a hurricane, and the believers began praising God in the native languages of the pilgrims attending the feast, languages the speakers had never learned. Some of the pilgrims were astonished, but some concluded that the believers were drunk (as if being drunk somehow sharpens our communication skills!). Because they waited and prayed, God worked through them in a truly miraculous way. In fact, the church was launched that day as the Spirit of God lived and worked through them.

But let's not get ahead of ourselves. We need to go back and think about what it meant for the disciples to wait. Have you ever been part of a ten day prayer meeting? Probably not. How about a ten hour prayer meeting? It would tax our brains and hearts to pray that long. For most of us, praying an hour is hard work. At some point during all those days, I can imagine the disciples saying to one another, "Hey, I've prayed long enough. Nothing's happened, or maybe what Jesus promised has already happened and I missed it. Whatever,

I'm going home to do something productive." Maybe that's what happened to the ones who bailed out and didn't wait.

Waiting is hard for us today because we live in an instant society and believe that we should never have to wait. We have ATMs all over town to dispense cash whenever we need it, we use drive-through windows for all kinds of things, and we cook with microwaves because we don't want to wait for the oven to bake our meals. A few generations ago when most people worked on farms, people had more patience with the slower patterns of life, but no longer. Most of us resent it when a line at the grocery store or the bank goes faster than the line we're in!

When we believe in the depths of our souls that we shouldn't have to wait, we complain, we doubt God's goodness, and we miss out on the lessons he wants to teach us. Some of the things we wait on aren't as trivial as a line at the grocery store. They're crucial to our health and happiness. We wait for an answer from the doctor after the CAT Scan. We wait for our child to finally respond positively to our loving correction. We wait for a spouse to care more about God and us than work, fishing, or basketball. We wait for God to answer a prayer for a loved one to come to faith. In a poignant scene, Isaiah tells us that God's people were tired of waiting on God. They complained, "My way is hidden from the LORD; my cause is disregarded by my God" (Isaiah 40:27). We may not use the same words, but our impatience with God carries the same perspective: "God, you've let me down. I counted on you, but it's like you're not even there. Thanks a lot." Isaiah patiently reminds the grumblers that though God may delay, we can still trust him. God's path for us may be difficult to understand, but we can trust him during times of delays if we remember that he is loving, attentive, wise, and powerful. In fact, while we wait, we have to dig deep into the character of God to trust him instead of giving in to pessimism.

Isaiah finishes his reminder to the people who hate to wait with a familiar but often misunderstood promise:

> *"But those who hope in the LORD*
> *will renew their strength.*
> *They will soar on wings like eagles;*
> *they will run and not grow weary,*
> *they will walk and not be faint" (verse 31).*

Some translations say, "Those who wait for the Lord will renew their strength." Many times in the Bible, the writers tell us to "wait for the Lord." Actually, the word wait in Hebrew means "to gather together." Waiting is God's way of bonding with us. The word renew is used two other times in the Old Testament to speak of someone "changing clothes." During delays, we consciously choose to take off our demands and doubts like a dirty shirt and put on the armor of faith. Strength is "God-given power, provision, and prosperity." With these definitions in mind, this passage means that those of us who bond with God will exchange our demands for a heart of confidence in his will and ways, and he'll give us everything we need to follow him and fulfill what he has called us to be and do. Occasionally we fly over our difficulties like an eagle, sometimes we run with endurance through them, but in a few excruciating instances, it takes all the faith we can muster just to keep putting one foot in front of the other. All of these, though, are examples of faith-filled waiting on God.

When we grasp God's purposes for delaying, we realize that waiting isn't about time; it's about producing a fervent expectation and deepening our dependence on God. We're sure God is going to act. We may not know how or when, but we trust in his character to come through according to his timetable. When we wait for a friend to join us for lunch, we have the sure expectation that he will show up. He may be late, but he'll arrive sooner or later. If he doesn't appear after twenty or thirty minutes, we don't conclude that he's irresponsible or thoughtless. If we know the friend is a trustworthy person, we imagine him stuck on the side of the road with no cell phone reception. In other words, because we trust the friend, we make positive assumptions about the unexpected delay. That's the message Isaiah communicated to the people who complained about God's delays.

If we cling to a steadfast trust in the goodness and greatness of God, we can endure delays—and even grow stronger in them. I believe God uses delays to accomplish three important purposes: to prepare us, to prepare others, and to prepare situations. If he moved more quickly, none of these things would be accomplished.

To Prepare Us

Quite often, the crucible of waiting is designed by God to work his grace more deeply in us. If he answered all our prayers immediately, we'd be like spoiled children who fly into tantrums when they're disappointed for any reason. In parenting, we try to instill the value of delayed gratification in our kids because we know it's essential to maturity. Should we expect anything different from our heavenly Father? Isaiah's message is a template for the lessons God wants to teach us while we wait. We learn to trust in his wisdom to lead us down the right path, in his goodness so that we develop a tenacious optimism even when we can't see the light at the end of the tunnel, and in his power to keep us strong as we wait for him to work. Throughout the Scriptures, we see people who had to wait for God to answer their prayers: Noah, Abraham and Sarah, Joseph, Moses, the prophets, and everyone else mentioned in Hebrews 11. Waiting, it appears, is one of God's primary instruments in shaping a mature faith in his people.

As we wait, we may find that God wants to work on our motivations. Maybe we want to see a miraculous answer to prayer so that others who are watching will think, "Man, he's terrific!" The discipline of waiting causes us to examine our hearts to see if we're more interested in the glory going to God or to ourselves. Sooner or later, we conclude, "God, it's not about me. It's all about you. I don't care about being praised. I just want you to be honored. I believe that you know the timing that will bring you the most glory, so I wait on you." At that point, but not before, God may open the door to his blessing.

To Prepare Others and Situations

In some instances, God uses delays to prepare the people and situations around us so that more lives will be affected when he explodes onto the scene. God could have sent the Spirit a moment after Jesus ascended or anytime during the ten days they prayed, but the pilgrims wouldn't have arrived in Jerusalem yet. He delayed the outpouring of the Spirit so they could hear the gospel in their own languages as the Spirit spoke through the believers on Pentecost. That's powerful timing and results!

One of the most important lessons in our spiritual lives is to see delays as God's classrooms and essential times of preparation. We're impatient people, but God is incredibly patient. We may think he's slow, but we can be sure that he's involved and intent on accomplishing his will in us. In times of waiting, we often experience confusion, emptiness, and silence. Without God's perspective on waiting, we might be like the 380 or so people who refused to wait and missed God's blessing. Our choice should be to cling to God through every moment of our lives—when he answers immediately or when he delays—and trust that his timing is right.

We may misunderstand the times of waiting while we're in the middle of them. We may think that we're waiting on a person to say "Yes" to us, an employer to hire us, a parent to show us the love we've always wanted, a friend to understand us without feeling compelled to fix us, or a prodigal child to repent and come home, but we really aren't waiting for people—we're waiting on God.

As we began a new year and a new decade at the start of 2010, we called our church to a season of prayer. One night each week for four weeks, about five hundred people came together to seek God and pour out their hearts about their faith, their families, their finances, and their future. On the last night, we came to a place in the prayer meeting where I felt God was about to speak to all of us in a special way. I told the people in the meeting, "Listen for God's leading. If he speaks to you a word that you think is for us, please come and tell me."

A few minutes later, a young lady came up to me and showed me her journal. She said, "Pastor Scott, God told me to show this to you. I think you'll be encouraged." She pointed to a page in her prayer journal where she had written weeks before: "For The Oaks: The time of struggle and waiting is over. You have been faithful, and I'm going to pour out my Spirit on you. You have been crying out to me, and now I'm going to answer you." I read her message to the people praying that night, and we erupted in praise to God. It seemed like I was living in that first scene in Acts. Weeks earlier God had given her a word for our church, but he told her to wait to share it. When the time was right, the Spirit poured out a huge blessing on all of us.

Peter (we'll see more of him tomorrow) wrote, "Humble yourselves, therefore, under God's mighty hand, that he may lift you up in due time. Cast all your anxiety on him because he cares for you" (1 Peter 5:6-7). Waiting requires humble faith, trusting that God will do what he wants to do "in due time"—that's his time, not ours. And when he's ready, we'll see him work, sometimes with a whisper but occasionally with the roaring wind. What does a good waiter in a restaurant do? He takes orders and serves. That's what a good spiritual waiter does, too. We take orders from God, and we keep serving him even during times when we don't see his hand or hear his voice. No matter what, we keep expecting God to come through in his way, in his time, for his honor. Expectant waiting is a normal part of the Christian life.

✚ **Read Acts 1:1-2:13.**

✚ **How do most people (maybe even you) react when they have to wait?**

✚ **When have you had to wait on God to come through for you?**

✚ **How well did you learn the lessons of waiting during that time?**

✚ **Is waiting more than just enduring delays? If so, what does it look like when we intentionally wait on the Lord?**

✚ **Complete the following prayer: "Jesus, you told the people on the hillside to wait, and you often tell me to wait. I want to learn the lessons you want me to learn. Today, I trust you to..."**

DAY TWO | **POWER UNLEASHED**

> "Then Peter stood up with the Eleven, raised his voice and addressed the crowd: "Fellow Jews and all of you who live in Jerusalem, let me explain this to you; listen carefully to what I say. These men are not drunk, as you suppose. It's only nine in the morning! No, this is what was spoken by the prophet Joel: 'In the last days, God says, I will pour out my Spirit on all people'""" (Acts 2:14-17).

Just fifty days before, Peter had denied he even knew Jesus when a servant girl confronted him as he warmed his hands over a fire. In the weeks after the resurrection, Jesus had met with him to restore their relationship, but I can imagine that Peter was still filled with doubt and shame over his colossal failure. Something significant, however, happened to him on the day of Pentecost. The Spirit of God confirmed Jesus' words of love, transformed him, and filled him with the power to speak boldly to the masses of people in the streets of Jerusalem. For Peter, the change couldn't have been more dramatic or complete.

When Peter stood up to talk about Jesus, he didn't just share his opinion. He related the prophesies of Joel, and told them about the promise of the resurrection in David's psalm. He boldly proclaimed Christ's death and resurrection as the hope of the world, and the Spirit wasn't working only in Peter's life. "When the people heard this, they were cut to the heart and said to Peter and the other apostles, 'Brothers, what shall we do?'" (Acts 2:37). That day, three thousand people repented and trusted in Jesus.

What had Peter been afraid of less than two months before? He had been terrified of being condemned alongside Jesus, so he lied and tried to hide his identity. What happened to transform him so that he now commanded the attention of thousands to proclaim an identity that he had denied so recently? It can only be explained by the filling of the Holy Spirit.

Many Christians in our churches do not understand the role of the Holy Spirit in their lives. Like some believers in Paul's day, they realize the Spirit led them to faith in Jesus, but they think they're on their own to figure out how to live for him each day. Fortunately, the Spirit's role is spelled out throughout the New Testament. He provides us with the necessities of spiritual life: the presence of God, the purpose of God, pardon for sins, and the power to live for Christ. Let's look at these.

Presence

If you and I had been in that room on Pentecost, or later in the streets as Peter proclaimed the message of Christ, we wouldn't have had any doubts about the presence of the Spirit. There was a rushing, mighty wind blowing through the room like a tornado. Fire fell from heaven, splitting into individual flames landing on each of their heads. They were praising God in languages they had never spoken before, and three thousand people were saved in a single altar call. The work of the Spirit was quite evident that day. The Spirit, as the third person of the Trinity, is omnipresent and continues to be at work in and through us today. He makes his presence known in a special way in the lives of believers. In an incredible display of humility, the awesome Presence of God has chosen to live inside each one of us who claims Christ as Savior. As an encouragement to turn from sin and live for God, Paul wrote, "Do you not know that your body is a temple of the Holy Spirit, who is in you, whom you have received from God? You are not your own; you were bought at a price. Therefore honor God with your body" (1 Corinthians 6:19-20). Where is God's Spirit at this moment? He is everywhere in the universe, and he has made his home in you and me. This concept is pretty awesome.

There are times when I sense the Spirit's presence, and it's not always in prayer. God breaks into my consciousness at odd times, when I'm praising and when I'm complaining, when I'm filled with compassion and when I feel annoyed by another's needs. From time to time, God whispers in my ear to remind me that I'm his and that he's called me to live for him. Paul described the whisper of the Spirit as a wonderful source of comfort: "For you did not receive a spirit that makes you a slave again to fear, but you received the Spirit of sonship. And by him we cry, "Abba, Father." The Spirit himself testifies with our spirit that we are God's children" (Romans 8:15-16). Over and over again throughout our Christian experience, God reminds us that we don't have a business relationship with him. We don't "gut out" the Christian life merely because we have to. We respond out of gratitude to God as our loving Father. In the depths of our hearts, he gives us confidence that we belong to him.

Purpose

The Holy Spirit's purpose is to bring honor to Jesus. As he works in us to give us love for God and compassion for others, he produces Christ's passion in us, and he empowers us to be his witnesses. Paul told the Corinthians that pleasing God is our "ambition." It's a strange word to find in the Bible, isn't it? We usually think of ambition as a sin, but it depends on the goal of the ambitious person. If our drive is to please the One who bought us, then ambition is good and right and acceptable. As we grow in our faith, our desires gradually begin to align with God's purposes. We care more about what he cares about. The things that break his heart break ours. We care about reaching the lost, not because we can put notches on our spiritual gun belts when a sinner repents, but because a lost person is found and an enemy of God becomes his friend. Touching lives is what the Spirit is all about. As we grow in our faith, we'll desire more and more to share the love, forgiveness, and strength of God with people in our own Jerusalem, as well as in our surrounding Judea and Samaria, even to the remotest parts of the earth.

Pardon

The Spirit's message is "pardon for sin and a hope that endures." Man's central problem is sin and separation from God; the only hope is the forgiveness Christ offers and the Spirit conveys to our hearts. It's not "just try harder and maybe God will accept you." Christ's forgiveness is the message Peter shared on that first day of the church's life, and it's the motivation for every believer to obey today. Some people think that forgiveness is only for special occasions, like the moment we come to faith and when we've hurt someone really badly. As we look at the Scriptures, though, we see that a deep and increasing understanding of forgiveness is essential to our spiritual growth.

Paul wrote, "For Christ's love compels us, because we are convinced that one died for all, and therefore all died. And he died for all, that those who live should no longer live for themselves but for him who died for them and was raised again" (2 Corinthians 5:14-15). How do we know how much Christ loves us? We know by continually looking at the cross. What kind of impact does Christ's love have on us? His love motivates us to choose God's will instead of selfishness.

Power

The message of the gospel contains propositional truth about the death and resurrection of Christ, but it doesn't remain on the page or in the air from the spoken word. Paul told the Romans, "I am not ashamed of the gospel, because it is the power of God for the salvation of everyone who believes" (Romans 1:16). The Spirit of God uses the word of God spoken by the people of God to radically transform hearts and destinies. Neither philosophy nor religious rules can do that. Only the Spirit's power changes lives. The power of the Holy Spirit sometimes is revealed in miracles and incredible harvests of souls like in Acts 2, but we see his power just as much when we pray, when God opens our hearts to understand his word, and when he gives us confidence to love the unlovely, turn the other cheek, forgive someone who hurt us, or offer the sacrifice of praise when we feel discouraged. All of these actions testify to the Spirit's power in us. We conclude, "No matter what I'm facing right now, I belong to the King of the universe, he is my loving Father who has adopted me as his own and I can trust him. He'll give me wisdom and strength to do his will."

When we see Peter speaking by the Spirit's direction and power in Acts 2, we see something very important: both his heart and message were saturated with God's word. He does not tell people his personal ideas and tack on a verse or two to sound spiritual. On the contrary, every word Peter spoke was shaped by the truth of Scripture or it was Scripture itself. A person's spiritual maturity is directly proportional to his understanding and application of God's word. In other words, we won't grow if we don't know the Bible.

We need to remember that the people who became the vessels of the Spirit's presence, purpose, pardon, and power were the same ones who had run away a few weeks before. Nothing we saw then could make us guess that this ragtag bunch, reacting with equal measures of doubt and arrogance, would become the people God used to change the world. When you and I wonder if we've got the right stuff, or if God could possibly use us to touch someone's life, we only need to remember the people of Pentecost. Some of the people in the streets that day were pilgrims visiting the city. They had stayed over from Passover to Pentecost. When the crowd heard the 120 telling the news of Christ in languages unfamiliar to them, many of the pilgrims may have wondered, "Aren't these the same people who were so terrified and sad a few weeks ago?" Yes, but something was different now—very different. Peter may have been a laughingstock for denying his leader to a servant girl, but now they saw that he had changed—incredibly changed. The Spirit works immediately and progressively. At the moment we trust Christ, the Holy Spirit enters our bodies and transfers our citizenship from the domain of darkness to the kingdom of God. He bears witness with our spirits (that's the whisper of assurance) that we belong to God. Then, for the rest of our lives, he works each day: through his word, in relationship with other believers who love us, in the good times and bad, to gradually transform us and conform us into the image of Christ.

The three thousand that believed Peter's message jump-started the church, but the Spirit wasn't through. Luke tells us that the believers couldn't keep the love of God from spilling out to every one they met. Every day, more people heard the good news, and every day more people trusted in Jesus.

In those first days, the Holy Spirit used Peter and other Christians to communicate the message to thousands of people. At that time, following Christ was a radical step—it still is. God's plan was for them to boldly proclaim Christ first in Jerusalem, and they were off to a great start.

I could share dozens of stories about times when I've shared the gospel, but one stands out as similar to that first day of Pentecost. Years ago, one of the students who led the Fellowship of Christian Athletes meeting at my son's high school asked me to speak to their local chapter. The topic the student asked me to address was "How to live for Christ without being a hypocrite." When I talked to the coach who served as the club's sponsor about the topic, he had reservations. "I don't know if it's a good idea to talk about that," he warned me. I guess he wanted me to talk about something less threatening than being sold out to Jesus. After we talked, I got nervous. I didn't want to offend anyone so I prayed and asked God to give me wisdom. I sensed very clearly that the Spirit wanted me to go for broke, share my heart, talk about forgiveness and obedience, and watch him work.

When I walked in the room, God gave me incredible compassion for the young men and women who came to the meeting. I loved them, and I wanted them to follow Christ with all their hearts. I spoke with authority and conviction, holding nothing back. I told them the story of Elijah and Elisha, and I asked, "Where are the people today who are willing to give everything to God?" I explained that we all are fallen, so we're all hypocrites, but we're only true hypocrites if we don't admit how much we need God's forgiveness and fail to respond to his love in obedience. Then, I talked about sex and God's design for a glorious sex life in marriage. There were forty-two students in the room that night. When I asked them if they wanted to trust in Jesus as their Savior, fifteen said "Yes" to Christ. I asked how many wanted to live full-out for the Lord, and twenty-five others stood up. I have no idea what happened in the lives of the other two, but I thought forty out of forty-two was pretty special.

This was my Jerusalem. Before I spoke, I knew that if I blew it, or if people were offended, it would hurt my reputation and the reputation of my boys who attended the school. But I trusted the Spirit to lead my preparation, guide my talk, and work with power in the hearts of these students to change their lives—and he did.

The next day at a ball game, a woman walked up to me and said, "My daughter was in the meeting with you last night." I didn't know which way this was going to go, so I just said, "Really?"

"Yes," she replied. "She told me all about your talk and especially the part about sex." I still wasn't sure what she was thinking, so I just nodded.

She continued, "My daughter told me that after listening to you, she's devoting her life to Christ, and has made a commitment not to have sex before she is married. She showed me the Scriptures you shared with the group, and we talked about them. I want you to know that what you talked about last night means a lot to my daughter, and it means a lot to me."

You might say, "Well, Scott, you're a pastor so you're paid to tell people about Jesus. I'm just a normal person." That may be true, but I could tell you countless stories about people who came to Christ because a normal, regular person had the courage to speak up about their faith. My friend Peter Haas was a Rave DJ in Minnesota. At one point in his life, he was so depressed that he didn't want to live any more. One day while he was at a gig, he walked outside for a smoke, and prayed, "God, I don't know if you're there, but if you're as big as people say you are, you ought to be able to show me. If you'll convince me that you're real, I'll follow you."

At that moment, a man he had never met walked up to him. He said, "I know this sounds strange because we've never met, but God asked me to tell you that Jesus loves you very much, and he wants you to trust him."

Amazed, he grabbed him by the arm and blurted out, "Tell me how! I need to know right now!"

The man was shocked, and thought Peter was making fun of him. He assured the man, "I'm not making fun of you at all. I just asked God to make himself real to me, and he's done that through you. I need your help." The man shared the forgiveness that could only be found in Jesus, and a heart was changed that day. Peter is now the pastor of a powerful church in Minneapolis, MN—all because a young man was obedient to the prompting of the Spirit.

Successful witnessing is sharing the message of Christ in the power of the Spirit and leaving the results to God. It doesn't mean that we won't feel afraid, and it doesn't guarantee that the person will respond in repentance. The power of the Spirit, though, enables us to overcome our fears and doubts so that we take steps to reach out and touch the lives of others. That's what happened in the opening scenes of Acts, it happened when that man had the guts to speak words of God's love to Peter Haas, and I believe it will happen as you and I invest in others. This is why I am so excited about the 50/50 challenge. As you give your 50 hours and $50 to care for those around you, the power of God's Spirit will be present and powerful to change lives—even your own.

When you reach out to people, don't be weird. The man who spoke to Peter Haas that day didn't wave his hands and pronounce loudly, "Thus saith the Lord!" No, he spoke words of kindness with humility in the context of the situation. Like him, let's use regular language with an understanding of our surroundings. Be bold, be gracious, be normal, and leave the person's response to God.

The Holy Spirit isn't some strange, magical power. He brings us to God, imparts the Father's love, honors Jesus, and transforms lives. He did that on the day of Pentecost, and he's still doing it today. It's normal to see him at work in and through us every day.

✚ Read Acts 2:14-41.

✚ What are some times in your life when you've sensed the Spirit's presence? How did that realization assure you?

✚ How do our purposes often conflict with God's? What would it be like for you to have the ambition to please him?

✚ Have you thought about how you want to invest your time and money as part of the 50/50 challenge? What has God been showing you? What's your next step?

✚ Complete the following prayer: "Spirit of God fill me, mold me, and use me. Today, I trust you to…"

DAY THREE | AS ONE

> "They devoted themselves to the apostles' teaching and to the fellowship, to the breaking of bread and to prayer. Everyone was filled with awe, and many wonders and miraculous signs were done by the apostles. All the believers were together and had everything in common"
> (Acts 2:42-44).

In those first weeks and months after Pentecost, believers experienced a powerful blend of thrills and threats that bound them in close relationships with each other. Throughout history—for over 4000 years—the Jewish culture has been established on strong bonds of interconnectedness. When God worked in those first days and thousands came to Christ, they were establishing a new community. Soon, however, the new Christians realized their Jewish neighbors and families didn't want them any more. They were outcasts among their own people. They lived under the threat that everything they had valued was turned upside down, everything they had known was now different, and everyone they had loved might now reject them. But they were thrilled to belong to Christ, to experience his love, forgiveness and power, and to belong to one another. They were creating a new family of God's redeemed children.

Jesus told the men on the hillside before he ascended to "teach [new believers] to obey everything I have commanded you" (Matthew 28:20). And now, in clusters on the Sabbath and in homes throughout the city, the disciples taught those who believed everything they had learned from Jesus. The Spirit continued to work miracles, and in a display of humility and love, people brought whatever they had to provide for those in need. Their love was so strong and the Spirit's power so evident that it's no wonder Luke tells us they were "praising God and enjoying the favor of all the people. And the Lord added to their number daily those who were being saved" (Acts 2:47).

The new believers in Jerusalem, however, weren't committed to unity—they were committed to Jesus, and he created unity when he worked in and through them in love. This is an important distinction. I've heard Christians complain about their small groups, churches, or other organization saying, "We just need to be more unified." This effort, however, almost always results in even more conflicts when people blame each other for not doing enough. Unity is achieved—and in fact, it thrives—when people focus their attention on Christ, not on themselves or their relationships.

Paul described the church as "the body of Christ." In his letter to the Ephesians, he said that our connection to each other is only as beautiful and strong as each person's connection is to Jesus. He wrote, "Speaking the truth in love, we will in all things grow up into him who is the Head, that is, Christ. From him the whole body, joined and held together by every supporting ligament, grows and builds itself up in love, as each part does its work" (Ephesians 4:15-16). Today, we know far more about the human nervous system than Paul did, but he knew that for a human body to function well, every part must get its directions from the head. Many churches and Christian groups today are unhealthy and display symptoms of cerebral palsy rather than a healthy body. The hands, feet, and other parts of the body jerk and move in seemingly random ways, and the person can't perform even the most basic functions of life. What causes these misfires in the body of Christ? There are several reasons we can identify:

1. We live in a disjointed culture. Today, the average person in our country moves 11.7 times in his or her lifetime. Each time the fabric of relationships is torn apart and a new one must be woven. We are the most mobile society the world has ever known, running from this place to that, day every day, with barely enough time to have more than superficial conversations.

2. We compete and compare. Modern media has had a dramatic impact on our expectations and relationships. The ads we see and hear almost every waking moment tell us that we can't be happy unless we have this product or that service, but even then, it's not enough. We have

to have a bigger house, a finer car, nicer clothes, and a better vacation than anyone else. If we would step back and look at the promises modern media offers us, we would recognize them as ridiculous lies. Unfortunately, we seldom take an honest look, and instead, buy the lies that ultimately destroy our relationships.

3. We insulate ourselves with wealth. There's nothing wrong with money or possessions. It's the love of these things that causes problems. In our culture, many of us use wealth (or the illusion of wealth by buying on credit) so we look like we don't need anyone or anything. We wear a mask of invincibility, which keeps us from being honest with God and with each other about our needs.

4. We're not good at resolving conflict. The Scriptures speak often and eloquently about the beauty of forgiveness in every relationship. We are thoroughly human, and we blow it in countless ways. We hurt others in big and small ways, and they hurt us in return. But instead of choosing to forgive, we harbor resentment, cherishing secret (or not so secret) thoughts of revenge. We excuse ourselves and blame other people, and with each day's resentment, another brick is put on the wall separating us from each other.

5. We spend our time and energy judging others instead of loving them. When we think we're better than others in God's family, we become self-righteous and critical. We may have an accurate perception about someone else's flaws, but we fail to notice the coldness in our own hearts. That was the sin of the Pharisees, and Jesus told them that they needed the faith of a child to enter his kingdom. Judging others according to our standards rather than the scripture's is the opposite of love and only serves to destroy unity.

These perceptions and corresponding behaviors are like faulty firing synapses in the nerves of a human body. They cause jerks and jolts, and they prevent the person from walking, talking, and performing necessary tasks that accomplish God's purposes in life. The problem, however, isn't corrected by simply trying to control all the jerks and twitches. The answer is to create new, workable pathways to the brain, and in our case, each person needs to be powerfully and fully connected to our Head, who is Christ.

What are the messages that course down the nerves from our Head? We don't have to look far in the Scriptures to see. Jesus said that his highest goal for each of us is to love God with all our heart, mind, and soul, and to love each other as we love ourselves. On these two directives, everything else hinges. If we are amazed by the love of God for us, blown away by his grace because we're thoroughly convinced that we don't deserve it, and thrilled that he has chosen us to be his children, then his love, forgiveness, and strength will flow out of us to those around us. We won't spend our time judging others for being different or acting weird. We'll show the same love for them that we enjoy: unconditional, free, and life changing.

Love for others in the body of Christ isn't something we manufacture or fake. It has to come from a genuine experience of God's love for us. John described it this way: "This is love: not that we loved God, but that he loved us and sent his Son as an atoning sacrifice for our sins. Dear friends, since God so loved us, we also ought to love one another" (1 John 4:10-11). The love of God can't pour out of us into the lives of those around us unless it first fills our hearts so much that it overflows. Unity, then, is a result of God's love spilling out of his people into the lives of those around them. We delight in Christ's amazing grace, and because we long to be like him, we give, serve, pray, and care for those he puts in our path. That's the source of unity, and it can only happen when God's people care more about him and each other than they do about their own wealth, position, or popularity.

When we fail to experience the overflow of God's love, we use people instead of caring for them. We may have connections, but they're designed for our pleasure and power, not to please Jesus. Unless we are submitted to Christ, we can't love people who are annoying, or forgive those who hurt us, or overlook others' strange habits. The people around us in God's family are not our competitors; they are brothers and sisters for whom Christ died, people he loves. When we are vitally connected to the Head his love fills our lives and we want all people to experience what God has for them. We're devoted to their good, not our pleasure. This kind of love is beautiful and inspiring as demonstrated in an act of generosity recently at our church.

A young man named Tim attended the Gathering, our church's young adult ministry. He met a man who desperately needed a car but didn't have the money to pay for it. The man and his wife had recently adopted three children so they wouldn't have to be put in Foster care. Because they only had an old pick up truck, they couldn't ride together without a couple of the kids sitting in their parents' laps. God directed Tim to give his SUV to this family—and he did. When the family drove away, they were incredibly grateful, but Tim had no idea what he'd do for transportation. He didn't know how he'd get to work, church, or anywhere else he needed to go, but the family's needs were more important to him than his convenience or the certainty of the future.

In the Gathering, we have a system for people to match needs and provisions. People can fill out cards saying "I need" or "I have." The next week, Tim attended the Gathering, wrote his need on a card, and put it in the offering. He simply wrote, "I need a car."

In a flash, a miracle happened. Ashley, a first-time guest at the Gathering, wrote on her card, "I have a car to give away." A few days later, she met Tim in the parking lot of the church to give him the keys to her car. Tim and his small group stood around the car rejoicing in God's provision and Ashley's generosity.

It was just like the believers in Jerusalem. The love of Jesus filled and overflowed from Tim's heart to provide for a needy family, so he gave his car away to people with a greater need. Then, only days later, God used Ashley to provide him with an even nicer car. Which was the greater blessing, to see the joy on the faces of the family driving the SUV he gave them, or to now have a better car than the one he gave away? If you asked Tim, the whole experience shouted the grace of God, but he was more thrilled to help a needy family. Still, he really appreciated Ashley's generosity and God's provision. Sometimes you have to surrender what you have before you can receive the next level that God has for you.

Tim and Ashley are perfect examples of what it means to experience unity in the body of Christ and give selflessly to those in need. As you think and pray about the 50 hours and $50, listen to the Spirit. Let him direct you, and then obey his whispered directions. God not only wants us to give what we have; he also wants us to give who we are to those in need. We give our hearts, our time, and our compassion as well as the tangible things we have in our possession. And sometimes, God wants us to give things we really need—not out of our surplus, but to the point where it hurts. When we think of how much Christ gave to us, there should be no limit to what we're willing to give back to him and to others in need. As Pastor Tommy Barnett often advised people in his church, "Find a need and fill it. Find a hurt and heal it." That kind of bold, loving action is normal for those who are connected to the Head and unified with one another.

⌗ **Read Acts 2:42-47.**

⌗ **Have you seen a group of believers so closely united with Christ that they became radically and beautifully unified with one another? If you have, describe their relationships. If not, what do you think this would look like.**

⌗ **What are some characteristics of unity in Luke's description of the early church? What would these look like today?**

⌗ **Which of the barriers to unity listed above seem to be the biggest challenges to you? How can you overcome them?**

⌗ **Complete the following prayer: "Jesus, I want to be so closely connected to you that your love spills out to everybody in my life. Help me overcome my resistance and the roadblocks. Today, I want to..."**

DAY FOUR | COMPASSION NOW

"Then Peter said, "Silver or gold I do not have, but what I have I give you. In the name of Jesus Christ of Nazareth, walk." Taking him by the right hand, he helped him up, and instantly the man's feet and ankles became strong. He jumped to his feet and began to walk. Then he went with them into the temple courts, walking and jumping, and praising God" (Acts 3:6-8).

In Luke's day, beggars and sick people often hung around the gates and pools of Jerusalem, some for many years. Luke tells us above about a man at the temple who had been crippled from birth, and for a long time he had made a meager living begging at the gate called Beautiful. Thousands of people passed him by during his life, and we can assume that in those early days of the church, many new believers had passed by him also. Perhaps they gave him a few coins as they went to worship. We can also assume that Peter and John had passed by him many times. This day, however, everything would change.

For some reason, Peter saw the man with a different set of eyes. He didn't just walk by or toss a coin in his hands. Peter stopped, looked at the man intently, and said, "Look at us!" The beggar may have thought, "Wow, I'm going to get some real money from this guy!" But money wasn't on Peter's mind.

Peter told him, "I don't have any money, but I have something far better to give you. In the name of Jesus Christ, stand up and walk!" The man hadn't asked to be healed, but Peter took his hand and helped him up. Luke tells us that he began walking and leaping and praising God. The message that day, however, wasn't just for him. "When all the people saw him walking and praising God, they recognized him as the same man who used to sit begging at the temple gate called Beautiful, and they were filled with wonder and amazement at what had happened to him" (Acts 3:9-10). Countless other people witnessed the miracle and believed. Never one to miss an opportunity to give a talk, Peter told the astonished crowd that it wasn't by his, or John's, power that accounted for the crippled man's transformation; it was Jesus. Like he had done at Pentecost, he explained the gospel to the people watching and listening.

Much like Peter and John, you and I pass by needy people each day. They have become part of our landscape, so familiar that we don't even notice them. But sometimes, God opens our eyes, our minds, and our hearts to see them. Suddenly, our hearts break with compassion, and we can't help ourselves. We may have been oblivious before, but no longer. We may have been preoccupied with our own desires before, but now their hurts and hopes break into our consciences. With a fresh realization of a desperate need, we do whatever it takes to step into a person's life to make a difference.

When we begin to notice one person's need, God often opens our hearts to notice more people and more needs. Recently, God has been working on me in this area, and has given me fresh eyes to see broken hearts all around me. Now, as I'm listening to the words people say, I'm also listening for the hidden meaning behind those words. For instance, I asked a friend a common (and often flippant) question, "Hey, how are you doing?"

He smiled and said, "Okay."

For my entire life up to that point, his answer would have been the trigger for me to assume he was doing just fine allowing me to feel free to pursue my agenda. This time, as God gave me new eyes and ears, I realized his "Okay" actually meant, "Scott, I'm really not doing okay, but I'm not sure I want to tell you what's going on because if I tell you and you don't really care, it'll devastate me. For that reason, I'll just stay on the surface."

That day, I said, "Hey, it seems like something's on your mind. Tell me what's going on?"

And he did. He told me that he was discouraged about his kids, and he wasn't enjoying his work. I asked him if he'd talked to anybody, and he shrugged, "Naw. Nobody wants to hear me complain."

"I do," I assured him. And it was the best talk we've ever had. When he told me more about his problems, I knew I didn't have to "fix" him. As we talked, he already knew what God wanted him to do, how God wanted him to trust him, and that he needed to exercise the power of radical gratitude to change his perspective. He just needed a friend to help him process his thoughts.

Each time I'm sensitive to the Spirit's whisper to listen to a person's heart, I become more in tune with the needs of people around me. A few days after my conversation with my friend, I was waiting to be seated at a restaurant with a friend of mine named Brian. I sat on a bench near a lady with two little boys. As I checked my voicemail, the younger boy, about three years old, came over and leaned on my leg. "What's that?" he asked as he poked his dirty little finger on one of the apps.

I wanted to say, "Hey, watch it kid!" but I quickly realized that this little boy might need some attention. I showed him how the phone worked and opened a few apps for him to see. He was mesmerized. I turned to his mother and asked, "Do you and your family live near here?"

She pointed to an older lady sitting nearby and replied to me, "My mother and my kids do." She paused for a second, realizing that I didn't understand, and then she explained, "I'm on duty in Iraq. Just home for a couple of weeks on leave."

Suddenly, I realized that her little boy was focused on me, not his mom. I looked more closely at this dear young mom, and it hit me that she felt distant from her two children. I quickly prayed, "Lord, help me." I got the little boy's attention and as he and his brother looked at me, I told both of them, "Little men, I want you to know something very important. Your mother is a genuine hero. She loves you so much, and she's a soldier in Iraq because she wants to be sure you're safe. I'm really proud of her, and I know you are, too."

The little boy immediately went over and gave his mom a big hug. His older brother sat a little closer to his mom and looked at her with love in his eyes. The lady looked at the two boys and hugged them, and then she looked at me and mouthed, "Thank you."

A minute later, Brian and I were called to our table. As we sat down, he asked, "Do you know what happened back there?"

I replied, "Yeah, I think I encouraged that mom and her kids."

"It was more than that," he told me. "My guess is that she gave birth to the younger child just before she was deployed, so that child has never known her. And from the looks of things, she's not married, so those boys don't have a man in their lives. Their grandmother is raising them the best she can. You affirmed their mother's role in their lives, and you affirmed her as a person. You gave her one of the most beautiful and powerful gifts she'll ever receive."

To be honest, I hadn't seen all that Brian saw, but I realized that if God gives me a little more perception, I'll be able to see much more into people's situations, speak timely words of hope and healing, and maybe provide some resources if they are needed.

To notice needs, I've been asking God to open my eyes, and I've asked Brian and a few others to be my mentors to help me read others' body language and really hear their spoken and unspoken messages. I'm realizing that there's far more meaning in what people say than their words often convey. As I become more sensitive to the Spirit and observant of people, I can help them take off their masks of self-protection and reveal a bit more of their hearts. Like me, most people have a dual, approach-avoidance way of relating to others. We desperately want others to know us, but we hide behind walls to prevent anyone from knowing the truth about us. No matter what a person's words are, if I sense tension, frustration, anger, or hurt, I'm learning to ask gently, "Hey, what's really going on?" I don't have to be a prophet or clairvoyant to read people's motives. That's not my role. I just want to be a friend. If I sense there's more going on than the person's words express, I ask about it. Sometimes, the person tells me everything about what's going on in their life, other times the response is simply, "I'd rather not talk about it." When that happens, I don't push or prod. I only say, "No problem. If and when you want to talk, I'm here."

In his grace, God uses our wounds and failures to make us more sensitive to others. Paul wrote to the Corinthians that Christ "comforts us in all our troubles, so that we can comfort those in any trouble with the comfort we ourselves have received from God" (2 Corinthians 1:4). Instead of despising our pain and hiding it, we can be assured that as God heals us, he'll make us sensitive to others who hurt and use us to bring hope and healing into their lives.

God sometimes opens our eyes to see people's needs when we least expect it. Donnie and Amy are students at Southwestern Assembly of God University in Waxahachie, Texas. One evening, they went on a date to see a movie. After the film as they were driving home, they saw an elderly woman stranded on the side of the road. Her car's hood was up, so they knew it was broken down. Donnie sensed that God was prompting them to stop, so he pulled over and asked if he could help. After they introduced themselves, the lady said her name was Marcia, and she'd been there for a long time hoping someone would stop to help her. For an hour Donnie tried to fix the car, but he couldn't figure out what was going on. Finally, he called a friend from school to bring his truck so they could tow the car to a mechanic.

While they were towing the truck, Amy took Marcia to a nearby fast food restaurant to get her something to eat. As they ate, Marcia opened her heart, telling Amy about the abusive home she grew up in, her drug addiction earlier in her life, her three divorces, and that her son was in prison. Amy's heart broke as she listened to Marcia's story. Amy prayed with her and shared her story of hope in Christ. She went out to the car and found a copy of The Next Level, a book about finding hope in hard times. While they waited on the mechanic to fix the car, Marcia and Amy talked until three in the morning.

Marcia didn't have a place to stay that night. She lived in Houston and was on her way to Ft. Worth. She couldn't reach anyone by phone, and she didn't have enough money for a hotel room, so Donnie invited her to stay at his house for the night. The next morning when Donnie got up, he found Marcia in the kitchen reading the book Amy had given her. She had been reading from the time they had gotten to the house, and was crying.

She told Donnie, "The message of this book is exactly what I need right now. I now understand why my life has gone the way it has. It's like God is talking to me—you and Amy stopping to help me, this book, both of you taking care of me. The love is overwhelming. Thank you so much!"

Later that morning Donnie and Amy took Marcia back to the mechanic's shop. When they got there, they found out it would cost $381 to fix her car. Donnie knew that Marcia didn't have that kind of money. He didn't know what to do, but God impressed him with the thought, "You pay it." For a few minutes, Donnie argued with God. He was just a university student, and he didn't have any money, but God reminded him, "Son, don't you think that I can take care of you?" Donnie quietly walked back into the office and gave the mechanic $381. The mechanic was shocked. He didn't understand why Donnie would be so generous to a complete stranger. He asked with a mixture of curiosity and bravado, "So kid, what's the deal?"

Donnie was tired, but he saw an open door. He shared the love of Christ with the mechanic, explaining that God is full of grace, and he loves people. Donnie told him that God had done so much for him that he wanted to "pay it forward" in a real and tangible way. The man was blown away—and so was Marcia when she came in and discovered that everything was paid for.

Marcia called Amy later and told her that the last two days had made an enormous impact on her. She told Amy, "I was leaving my family. Actually, I was running away, but now I'm going back home. God stopped me on the side of the road and sent you and Donnie to help me. I can't thank you enough." She explained that the mechanic had told her that Donnie had paid the bill for the repairs. She said, "I cried then, and I'm crying again now just thinking about how kind you both have been to me. Because of you, I'll never be the same."

Later, Amy told me this story and reflected, "Pastor, I'm so excited about what happened that night and the next day. Who knew God would work so much in a person's life just because we felt impressed to stop and help? It's amazing!"

Needy people are all around us—at home, at work, in our neighborhoods, in school, on the streets, and sitting next to us in church. Not every needy person, however, is a mandate for ministry. If we felt compelled to meet every need, we'd become obsessive compulsive, burdened with guilt, and would soon burn out. That's not the abundant Christian life! Sometimes, God needs to prepare a person's heart before he opens our eyes to a need, and sometimes, he wants to prepare us. When the time is right, we need the Spirit of God to open our eyes to see beyond other people's masks and open our ears so we learn to hear what their hearts are really saying. Then, we can step in and become vessels for the Spirit's power to change lives. If we're willing, God will direct us and use us to step into people's needs. Being God's instrument of healing and hope will become a normal part of our lives.

⨁ **Read Acts 3:1-19.**

⨁ **What are some reasons why we don't usually notice the needs of others? What excuses have you used recently to avoid the risk and expense of helping someone else?**

⨁ **In what way does God use our hurts to produce compassion in us for others? How have you seen him do that in your life?**

⨁ **What are the benefits of noticing people's needs? What are some of the risks?**

⨁ **Complete the following prayer: "Jesus, you noticed my needs, and you stepped into my life to meet them. Today, help me see and hear more clearly than ever before. Help me to…"**

DAY FIVE | **BOLD AS A LION**

"Then they called them in again and commanded them not to speak or teach at all in the name of Jesus. But Peter and John replied, "Judge for yourselves whether it is right in God's sight to obey you rather than God. For we cannot help speaking about what we have seen and heard" (Acts 4:18-20).

It all began so innocently. Peter and John were on their way to the temple to pray, but the Spirit had another agenda for them. Peter saw a crippled man begging at the temple gate, who he'd seen dozens of times in the past. But, now full of the Spirit, Peter saw him with new eyes. He told the man to rise up in the name of Jesus and instantly the crippled man was healed. A crowd of people gathered to see the spectacle as the "crippled" man danced around praising God. Peter used the occasion to tell everyone who would listen about Jesus. Wherever the gospel is proclaimed, however, opposition arises—in a home, a school, at work, in neighborhoods, and across the oceans in other lands. While Peter was talking about Jesus, he caught flack. Luke tells us, "The priests and the captain of the temple guard and the Sadducees came up to Peter and John while they were speaking to the people. They were greatly disturbed because the apostles were teaching the people and proclaiming in Jesus the resurrection of the dead. They seized Peter and John, and because it was evening, they put them in jail until the next day" (Acts 4:1-3).

The authorities felt threatened. Why? They hated the message, but even more, they realized they were losing their place of leadership with the people. That day at the temple, thousands believed Peter's message about the forgiveness and hope they could find in Christ.

The rest of the story about this event is almost comical. The leaders of the Sanhedrin, the most powerful legislative and religious body in the Jewish nation, dragged Peter and John, two poor fishermen in front of them to be interrogated about the awesome power God displayed through them. Peter may have realized the predicament he was in—he and John could be excommunicated from the temple, outcasts in a culture that highly valued inclusion—but he didn't back down an inch. He was filled with the Spirit, and he announced boldly, "Rulers and elders of the people! If we are being called to account today for an act of kindness shown to a cripple and are asked how he was healed, then know this, you and all the people of Israel: It is by the name of Jesus Christ of Nazareth, whom you crucified but whom God raised from the dead, that this man stands before you healed" (Acts 4:8-10).

The sides were clearly drawn: the old, established powerbrokers who had a vested interest in eliminating any changes in the existing structure against a couple of uneducated fishermen who were, by the way, filled with the Spirit of God. It was no contest. Luke tells us, "When they saw the courage of Peter and John and realized that they were unschooled, ordinary men, they were astonished and they took note that these men had been with Jesus. But since they could see the man who had been healed standing there with them, there was nothing they could say" (Acts 4:13-14). Living by the power of the Spirit, these two guys were as bold as a lion!

Like little children throwing a tantrum because they felt out of control, the religious leaders threatened Peter and John, "You'd better not do this again!" But Peter answered with a blend of faith and diplomacy: "Judge for yourselves whether it is right in God's sight to obey you rather than God. For we cannot help speaking about what we have seen and heard."

Actually, my favorite part of this story comes next. The religious leaders released Peter and John who returned to the believers, and together, they prayed and celebrated God's power. They asked God to work powerfully through them so that even more people would trust in Jesus. How did God respond to their prayer for bold faith? "After they prayed, the place where they were meeting was shaken. And they were all filled with the Holy Spirit and spoke the word of God boldly" (Acts 4:31).

What's the difference between Peter and John's boldness to tell people about Jesus whatever the cost . . . and our, often tepid, efforts to share our faith? A few brave people around the world, including our community, are willing to stand up for Christ and endure insults, estrangement, and even death for the gospel, but many of us find excuses to keep our mouths shut. Let me mention a few of the most common reasons why people aren't as bold as they could be:

1. Lack of knowledge of how to communicate the gospel clearly. We're afraid someone will ask a hard question, and we'll look stupid.

2. Fear of rejection. Most of us don't fear arrest, imprisonment, or death, but we're afraid our friends won't accept us anymore if we speak up about our faith in Jesus.

3. Social awkwardness in initiating a conversation about Jesus. If somebody asks about our faith, we're happy to tell him, but if not, we keep our mouths shut.

4. Fear of suffering genuine ridicule for the faith. When a boss finds out an employee is a Christian, he makes it his life's purpose to make the believer's job—and his entire life—miserable. He gives him the worst assignments, writes up scathing reports about his work even though it has been exemplary, and openly laughs at his faith in front of others at staff meetings.

5. The thought that there are "more important" things on our agenda than telling people about Jesus. It's simply inconvenient to get involved in these discussions.

We can come up with all kinds of creative excuses for not telling people about Christ, but all of them miss an important truth: the stark reality of eternity. People in our culture live for pleasure, possessions, and prestige. In fact, they expect heaven on earth. God sometimes orchestrates difficulties to shake people out of their misguided expectations and reveal their need for a Savior. The gospel provides hope for now and for all eternity. There will come a day when every person will stand before God. If we're gripped with that reality, we'll look beyond our excuses and the apathy of people to speak grace and truth into their lives. Seeing people through the lens of eternity makes all the difference in building a reservoir of boldness in our souls. In his famous sermon, "The Weight of Glory," C. S. Lewis observed that an eternal perspective shows us there are "no ordinary people." He said, "It is a serious thing to live in a society of possible gods and goddesses, to remember that the dullest and most uninteresting person you talk to may one day be a creature which, if you saw it now, you would be strongly tempted to worship, or else a horror and a corruption such as you now meet, if at all, only in a nightmare. All day long we are, in some degree, helping each other to one or other of these destinations. It is in the light of these overwhelming possibilities, it is with the awe and the circumspection proper to them, that we should conduct all our dealings with one another, all friendships, all loves, all play, all politics. There are no ordinary people. You have never talked to a mere mortal."

On the day of the crucifixion, it appeared that the power of evil and the religious establishment had won. Jesus was dead and buried. But a few days later, everything changed. The power of the resurrection gave hope to the hopeless and turned a bunch of discouraged, demoralized men and women into lions of the faith! Now, when Peter and John were arrested and accused for healing a man in the name of Jesus, they were thoroughly convinced that a new reality trumped anything they had ever believed before. When they prayed, they didn't back down, and they didn't even ask for protection. Look at the power of their prayer: "Indeed Herod and Pontius Pilate met together with the Gentiles and the people of Israel in this city to conspire against your holy servant Jesus, whom you anointed. They did what your power and will had decided beforehand should happen. Now, Lord, consider their threats and enable your servants to speak your word with great boldness. Stretch out your hand to heal and perform miraculous signs and wonders through the name of your holy servant Jesus" (Acts 4:27-30). I love this prayer. They were saying, "God, you orchestrated this whole thing. You are sovereign, and no one can stop your plan. And now, we don't want to back up at all. We're going to keep speaking out boldly, and we ask you to confirm our message with miracles so nobody can deny your power, authority, and grace!"

As we'll see in the next few chapters, the Sanhedrin's threats weren't empty ones. Christians were arrested, stoned, killed with a sword, and abused in many other ways. Peter, John, and the rest of the believers displayed boldness in the face of genuine risks to their freedom, their reputations, and their lives. After all, the authorities had killed Jesus only weeks before.

We can learn a lot from the example of believers in foreign lands where the gospel is seen as a threat to the government. Karolina is a fifth-grade student in Belarus who trusted God for boldness. Here's her story in her own words.

One autumn day we all came to school. In the first class, our social teacher started speaking about different youth organizations, and her favorite was BRSM (Belorussian Republican Youth Union). She said it helped old people, made our city greener, and assisted young people in living a healthy life (though they also provided fake certificates to enable them to buy alcohol and go to nightclubs). What she didn't mention was that BRSM also was a political organization and was created by a collaboration of the Belorussian Patriot Youth Union and Lenin's Communist Youth Union. The BRSM is, in fact, a communist organization.

My parents have always expressed their gratitude to God that the Soviet Union fell down because that was a real curse for our country. My parents were so poor that they had to save money to buy one banana for me twice a year. And the communists hated my parents' faith. The party denies the existence of God, and has actively persecuted pastors and church leaders for their faith. I'm a Christian, and I couldn't keep silent while others were being forced to be involved in BRSM. In class, I tried to ask some questions, but the social teacher ignored me. When she left the room, I started a big discussion with our classmates. I told them everything I knew about God, and God gave me wisdom. I said, "You do not need an organization to do good things, but if you do, then certainly don't get involved in BRSM." We all agreed on it!

The next day the social teacher came to give us forms to join BRSM. Somebody told her, "Sorry, but nobody is going to join BRSM in our class." I don't know if the social teacher asked anybody why, but someone told her that I had told them not to join. Later, when I was at my geography lesson, the director of studies came in and asked, "Is Karolina Goncharenko here?" Everybody looked at me and pointed. "Come with me," she said. I went out of the classroom and asked what had happened. She answered, "You would not be afraid if you hadn't done something wrong!" By her face and voice I could judge that she was sure I had.

We entered the principal's room. He was sitting at the table, and the second director of studies was next to him. He started to speak in a loud voice, "I've heard that you dissuaded the whole class! What's the matter with you?"

He was beating the table with his fists. "It doesn't matter that you're the best pupil in the class. I will banish you out of school! And I will talk to your father to tell him what you've done."

I tried to say something, but I couldn't. I went out of his room and started to cry. What wrong had I done? Why couldn't I say what I think about God? I called my mom and told her everything. When I went back to my geography lesson, everyone stared at my red, tear-stained face. In about ten minutes, the headmaster and both directors of studies came in. The headmaster said, "Children! You must join BRSM! Do not listen to anybody. We've already talked to her, right, Karolina?" I answered nothing. As they left, tears ran out of my eyes again. In the end, only two or three people from our class entered BRSM, while in others classes almost everybody joined. Later the headmaster told my dad that they must have eighty percent participation at school, otherwise they all will be fired. When I heard that I said, "Let my class be the twenty percent." Before long, the school leadership was imprisoned for not reaching the eighty percent enrollment. But at least most of the children in my class stayed out of the BRSM.

You and I may have an obstinate sibling or parent, a defiant neighbor, or a scoffing friend. If Karolina was willing to put herself and her family on the line to share her faith and take a bold stand against the forces of evil, how far are we willing to go in our much safer environment? What price are we willing to pay? Christians in some parts of the world face arrest or expulsion from college because of their faith. Are we willing to endure a raised eyebrow, or a shift in our convenience to carve out time for a conversation about Jesus? For most of us, the price isn't much more than that. No matter what price must be paid, we have to look at the reality of eternity for the people around us and ask, "Is it worth it?"

Boldness for Christ doesn't come out of a vacuum. If we just try to manufacture intensity, zeal, and passion, these emotions will wane sooner or later. The tenacity of Peter and John was rooted in their deep understanding of God's greatness and grace, as well as their own experience of personal transformation. Boldness came from heartfelt convictions of the sovereignty of God, the sacrifice of Christ, and the filling of the Spirit. They saw past the roadblocks of the religious leaders into the hurting hearts of men and women. They cared more for God and the destinies of other people than for their own comfort.

The lessons for us are clear. God has put us in relationships for a purpose. They are not by accident, nor are they a mistake. God has sovereignly planted us in places where we can make a difference in people's lives—but only if we speak up and shine the light of the gospel by our attitudes and actions. When we speak up about Christ, we can expect a range of responses, from joyful repentance to outright hostility. As we think, plan, and pray about the impact God wants to have through us, we ask him for new eyes to see there are "no ordinary people"—we are all creatures with an incredible destiny. And we pray for boldness, not protection, so that we can speak the words of grace with joy, clarity, and effectiveness. If we're confused or afraid, we can do what Peter and John did: we can call our friends to pray with us and for us. We can be confident that the Spirit of God will work in and through us to enable us to do exactly what Jesus instructed us to do—to be his witnesses in our own Jerusalem, Judea and Samaria, and to the remotest parts of the planet.

Be bold, be humble, be strong, and trust God to use you to change lives.

✚ **Read Acts 4:1-31.**

✚ **How does understanding there are "no ordinary people" give you compassion for the lost people all around you? Do they matter to God? Do they really matter to you? Why or why not?**

✚ **What are some reasons and excuses you use to keep from telling more people about Christ? How valid are they?**

✚ **Who are two or three people you want to tell about Christ? Who can you enlist to pray for you? How do you want them to pray?**

✚ **Complete the following prayer: "Jesus, you're worthy of my boldness, and people around me desperately need you. Help me today to…"**

DAY SIX
OPEN HEARTS, OPEN HANDS

"All the believers were one in heart and mind. No one claimed that any of his possessions was his own, but they shared everything they had. With great power the apostles continued to testify to the resurrection of the Lord Jesus, and much grace was upon them all. There were no needy persons among them. For from time to time those who owned lands or houses sold them, brought the money from the sales and put it at the apostles' feet, and it was distributed to anyone as he had need" (Acts 4:32-35).

Generous living isn't about the money or the possessions; it's about the significance of the cause. Luke reminds us again that in the early days of the life of the church believers were so captured by the cause of Christ that they were willing to do anything—anything!—to help people come to faith and grow closer to Jesus. In our case, the cause isn't just reaching every person with the gospel—the cause is Christ himself. Certainly, world evangelism is an incredibly valuable goal, but we have something more compelling and more beautiful to shape our motivations: Jesus. In his prayer the night he was arrested, Jesus said, "Now this is eternal life: that they may know you, the only true God, and Jesus Christ, whom you have sent" (John 17:3). We are driven and drawn to please the One who has demonstrated his love for us by paying the ultimate price. Please don't misunderstand. I'm not denigrating the cause God has called us to join. It's the most challenging, all-encompassing cause the world has ever known, but there's a higher, deeper, wider motivation than merely accomplishing a great goal or facing a huge challenge. It's the ambition to please Jesus.

As the believers in the early days of the church experienced the presence and power of Jesus, they delighted in being his and participating in his work with him. Their attitude was, "Jesus, I'm yours. Every part of me, everything I own, and everything I'll ever be, I'm all yours." They were so enamored by Christ that they couldn't imagine holding anything back. They were, Luke tells us, "one in heart and mind." When God captures a person's heart, he opens his hands to give generously. That's what happened to the believers. Those who had resources gladly provided for those who had none. In a remarkable statement, Luke tells us, "There were no needy persons among them. For from time to time those who owned lands or houses sold them, brought the money from the sales and put it at the apostles' feet, and it was distributed to anyone as he had need" (Acts 4:34-35). One of those who sold lands and gave money to the poor was a man named Barnabas. We'll hear a lot more about him later, but for now, all we need to know is that he put everything he owned in God's hands to provide for needy believers.

In this story, though, we find another couple. Their motives were very different. Undoubtedly, Ananias and Sapphira saw how people appreciated the generosity of Barnabas and others who sold property and donated the money to the church, so they hatched a plan. They sold property and brought part of the money to the apostles, claiming they were giving the entire purchase price, but Peter found out about the deception. The problem, he told Ananias, wasn't that he kept some of the money. The problem was his self-absorbed motive and his attempt to lie to God and to God's people. Peter told him, "Ananias, how is it that Satan has so filled your heart that you have lied to the Holy Spirit and have kept for yourself some of the money you received for the land? Didn't it belong to you before it was sold? And after it was sold, wasn't the money at your disposal? What made you think of doing such a thing? You have not lied to men but to God" (Acts 5:3-4).

Ananias fell over dead, and a few minutes later, his wife confirmed her part in the conspiracy, and she too breathed her last. What can we learn from this important moment in the life of the church? Was it harsh of God to slay those two who had given only a portion of their money to him? Don't you and I give a portion each time we give? What's the difference?

The problem was their motive, not the size of their check. They were giving, not to honor Christ or to further the kingdom, but to win applause from people who were watching. The lesson wasn't new to the people who had heard Jesus teach. They remembered that he told them, "Be careful not to do your 'acts of righteousness' before men, to be seen by them. If you do, you will have no reward from your Father in heaven. So when you give to the needy, do not announce it with trumpets, as the hypocrites do in the synagogues and on the streets, to be honored by men. I tell you the truth, they have received their reward in full" (Matthew 6:1-2).

If God, or Peter, had winked at their deception, the church would have gotten off to a terribly destructive start. Hypocrisy is the antithesis of integrity. A strong, vibrant faith can't grow where hypocrisy is tolerated. If we look at the discussions Jesus had with the religious leaders, we'll see that many of his fierce condemnations concerned this same issue. They talked a good game, and loved "respectful greetings" and the trappings of power in their culture, but their hearts were far from God. Now, when two people in the church threatened to infect the new community with this disease, God made sure it was stopped cold. As they carried the couple out to the cemetery, "Great fear seized the whole church and all who heard about these events" (Acts 5:11). People concluded rightly, "Wow, this is really serious! God not only cares about what I do, but why I do it. I'd better examine my motives and trust God to clean them up."

When you and I participate in giving our 50 hours and $50, we need to examine our hearts. If we're doing it to win acclaim from people who are watching, we need to be honest and repent. The problem wasn't that Ananias and Sapphira had sinful, selfish thoughts about what they could do with their money; it was that they acted on those sinful, selfish thoughts. If they had repented while they had the money in their hands, they would have been listed with generous giants like Barnabas. Repentance—at whatever point we realize our motives stink—pleases God and frees us from crushing guilt.

Is the lesson of this story that we shouldn't tell people what we've done to honor God? If our goal is to promote ourselves, we need to stay quiet and give, serve, and pray in secret for the audience of One instead of the applause of many. But if our heart's desire is to honor God and tell what he's doing in and through us, we can humbly share our story with joy and passion. Can you tell the difference? We shouldn't go around judging people's motives, but we are called to examine our own. If I'm shading the facts so they appear a little more dramatic, I can be sure I'm focused on promoting my reputation, not God's glory. If I linger and ask for a response of appreciation after I've shared my story, it shows that it's too much about me, not him. We're all "in process," and we'll have somewhat tainted motives until we see Jesus face to face, but we can't let this fact be an excuse for letting sinful desires control our lives. We can repent at any point when we become aware that our motives are impure and self-promoting. Then we can bask in God's forgiveness and make choices to honor him in all we say and do.

False humility, though, is just as destructive as blatant pride. When we fail to speak up about what God is doing because we "don't want to call attention to ourselves," it sounds noble and spiritual, but this approach can also be all about us instead of him. It's perfectly good and fine to tell people what God is up to in our lives if we delight in him and enjoy shining the spotlight of fame on him. I'm thrilled when God chooses to use me—even me—to touch somebody's life. There's nothing wrong with that kind of pleasure.

When we close our hearts to God and to generosity, we, too, experience a kind of death—not the kind Ananias and Sapphira experienced, but a coldness toward God and people. We spend our time hoarding what we have and thinking about getting more, not daydreaming about how God might use what we have for his glory. We don't want to pray too long because we're afraid that God might whisper something to us that we don't want to hear. That's not the way we want to live. Instead of hiding from the Spirit, we want to be completely open to him and his guidance with everything we've got.

We've developed a tradition at our church called "Christmas at The Oaks." We realized that people often give generously at that time of year, but they seldom see how their money impacts individuals and families. I explained to our people that each Sunday for three weeks before Christmas, we'd pass the regular offering plate, and then we'd pass the Red Bucket for them to put in cash for people in need. In one service, I looked at a dear family I know, and I said, "See the Stanleys over here? If they knew that a family needed $80 for groceries this week, they'd be thrilled to give them the money. The problem is that they don't know the family I know who needs that money. Do you see the Coles? If they realized that another family needs $120 for winter jackets for their three kids, they'd give that money in a heartbeat. But they don't know that family. The Stanleys and Coles, and other families in the church like them, have three things in common: a heart for God, a love for people, and the means to give. We're going to use the Red Buckets to connect them with people in need."

The cash in the Red Bucket wasn't for people to pay for a new car or for any other luxury. I told people, "If you're wondering how you're going to buy groceries or get a jacket for your child, I want you to take just as much money as you need from the bucket. If you need $43.27, take that much out, but not a penny more—but don't take any less either." I know people, and I was sure that some needy people would be reluctant to come up and get the money they needed. I told them, "I know what some of you're thinking. You don't want to come up and take money out of a box because you're too proud to let anyone know you're in need. Well, I have something to say to you: Get over it!"

In each service, our ushers took up both offerings—the regular one and the Red Bucket offering—and they brought the buckets up to the front of the church and poured out the cash into nicely wrapped boxes. We wanted them to look like Christmas presents. We didn't count the money, and we didn't portion out a certain amount for each box. It was entirely random. I invited people who needed money to come down front. Our deacons stood with each of the boxes to help people count out the exact amount they needed. It was a beautiful thing to see.

Since we didn't count the money in the Red Buckets, we're not sure how much money was donated and taken. We estimated it was about thirty-five thousand dollars for the three weeks. By the last week, people had overcome their fear and pride, and scores of them came down to get the money they needed.

Some people took more than they should, and some took less than they really needed. As I prayed about what was going on, the Lord reminded me that this is always what happens when grace is extended. It's always messy, but it's always beautiful.

Before the last week, I asked the Lord what he wanted us to do about the future of the Red Bucket. Several people had asked if we were going to make this a regular part of our worship experience. As I prayed, I sensed that God told me that we should make the Red Bucket a regular part of our individual lives, to give generously out of a heart of gratitude. Before I got up to speak the next Sunday morning and explain this perspective, a man came up to me. He looked a little disturbed. He said, "Pastor, I don't have money for the Red Bucket this morning. I'm sorry about that."

I patted him on the shoulder, "That's no problem."

He explained, "I had it when I left the house, but I met somebody when I arrived in church this morning, and I felt God was telling me to give the money to her. I hope that's okay."

"Brother," I beamed, "that's exactly the message God put on my heart this morning. The Red Bucket concept isn't going to die. God wants it to stay in our hearts. He wants to take it viral!"

In many ways, that's what this book is about. The 50 hours and $50 are a way of making the Red Bucket a normal part of our life of faith. We're always on the lookout to see who needs a touch of God's kindness, and we're always ready to be an instrument in his hands to meet a need, heal a hurt, and give hope to the hopeless. Open hands, however, begin with an open heart. We first are overwhelmed with the matchless grace of God, and we gladly tell him, "I'm all yours, God. I'm thrilled for you to use me any way you choose!" It's normal for us to continually grow in our ability to respond to the needs around us with openness and generosity.

⊹ **Read Acts 4:32-5:11.**

⊹ **How do you think the events of the healing of the crippled man, Peter's sermon with thousands responding to Christ, the arrest and trial, and the ground-shaking prayer meeting affected people's willingness to be generous with their possessions?**

⊹ **Describe a time when you were thrilled to give something of value to you to someone in need.**

⊹ **What would it mean for you to have a "Red Bucket" lifestyle?**

⊹ **Complete the following prayer: "Father, you've given me so much. I want your love to overflow from me to help people around me. Lead me today to…"**

DAY SEVEN | FAITHFUL

"Peter and the other apostles replied: 'We must obey God rather than men! The God of our fathers raised Jesus from the dead—whom you had killed by hanging him on a tree. God exalted him to his own right hand as Prince and Savior that he might give repentance and forgiveness of sins to Israel. We are witnesses of these things, and so is the Holy Spirit, whom God has given to those who obey him.' When they heard this, they were furious and wanted to put them to death"
(Acts 5:29-32).

You'd think that religious leaders would be overjoyed to see crippled people healed, the blind seeing, the sick restored to health, and evil spirits cast out of those who had been cruelly possessed, but instead, they were furious! Jealousy is an ugly thing. It destroys relationships, and it poisons the hearts of those who let it seep into their souls. It turns reasonable people into maniacs and kind people into tyrants. That's what happened to the religious leaders who watched God work through the unschooled, uncouth country bumpkins and misfits who were leading the new (and growing) community of Christians.

The events Luke describes in this chapter of Acts is much like the earlier account of the arrest of Peter and John after they healed the crippled man at the gate Beautiful. Why did Luke include similar stories? Because they both happened, and he wanted us to get the picture that living for Christ brings out the best and worst in our experience. Because the disciples were tenaciously faithful to God, the Lord poured out his Spirit to work in incredible ways.

How powerful was the testimony of the early believers? Luke records two dramatic statements. He said the people were in such awe of the new community of Christians that "all the believers used to meet together in Solomon's Colonnade. No one else dared join them, even though they were highly regarded by the people" (Acts 5:12-13). What an amazing level of respect! But that's not all. We also learn: "People brought the sick into the streets and laid them on beds and mats so that at least Peter's shadow might fall on some of them as he passed by. Crowds gathered also from the towns around Jerusalem, bringing their sick and those tormented by evil spirits, and all of them were healed" (Acts 5:15-16).

As the religious leaders saw what was happening, they became jealous, and again, they tried to stop them from talking about Jesus. They arrested the apostles (all of them, we can assume), and threw them in jail. During the night an angel appeared and brought them out. At dawn, there they were again, preaching about Jesus in the temple. Can you imagine how upset the high priest, the Pharisees and Sadducees were? They were livid—confused, but livid. They sent the temple guard to round them up, but this time, they dared not use force because they were afraid the crowd would stone them. The power structure of Palestine was undergoing a tectonic shift.

Again, the high priest and his associates threatened the apostles. He complained, "We gave you strict orders not to teach in this name. Yet you have filled Jerusalem with your teaching and are determined to make us guilty of this man's blood" (Acts 5:28).

I can almost hear Peter thinking, "That's the point!" But he said, "We must obey God rather than men!" And again, he told the high priest the message of the cross.

The high priest was so angry that he wanted to kill all of them, but a brief conversation with a trusted leader convinced him to let the apostles go. Before they walked out, though, he had them flogged, just like the Romans had flogged Jesus a few weeks earlier. Were the apostles upset? Did they complain that they didn't deserve such awful treatment? Not at all, instead they rejoiced "because they had been counted worthy of suffering disgrace for the Name" (Acts 5:41). The contrast of the responses in this part of Luke's story is striking, but it still happens today. Wherever the gospel is proclaimed and Christians love people in their communities, some respond with belief and others with disgust. I've seen it most often in families.

My friend Ray told me that his parents tried to explain away his faith in Christ by telling their friends he had been brainwashed and had joined a cult. But Ray had found spiritual vitality at college that was similar to the early days of the church. He was drawn to a group of believers because they didn't just say they loved people, they actively demonstrated their care for them. When they prayed, it wasn't like the empty, formulaic prayers he had heard in church when he was a boy. They were really talking with God, and he was listening! They gave whatever they had to help anyone in need: people of different races and economic backgrounds. For years, Ray had stayed away from Christians because they seemed either phony or weird, but this group of believers was authentic—their love for God and for people was the real thing.

During Ray's senior year, the campus organization of believers planned a Good Friday event, but that morning, the heavens opened up and a drenching storm flooded the campus. It didn't look like it would ever quit. Ray met with some of the students who had worked so hard to bring two professional football players to speak that day, and they prayed. I mean, they really prayed. They asked God to stop the rain so they could proclaim his name to the other students on campus. Ray remembered, "To be honest, I looked up at them while we were praying, and I thought, 'Man, this is nuts. There's no way that rain is going to stop.' " The meeting was scheduled for noon on the wide sidewalk outside the student union. He remembers, "At 11:50 a.m. the rain stopped, the clouds parted, and the sun came out. We hurriedly set up a microphone, and the athletes shared their testimonies about Christ. Hundreds of students sat on the wet pavement to listen. I just sat there—with my butt soaking wet—looking around at all the people listening to the gospel. After about thirty minutes, one of the football players invited people to pray to receive Christ, and the meeting was over. Within five minutes, the clouds came back and the rain poured down again." He reflected, "There's no way anybody can tell me this wasn't a miracle. God was at work that day. He wanted somebody to hear the gospel, and he moved heaven and earth to make it happen. Pretty cool."

In his second letter to the Corinthians, Paul describes the contrast in responses when we talk about Jesus. Everybody, Paul explains, thinks we smell. He wrote, "But thanks be to God, who always leads us in triumphal procession in Christ and through us spreads everywhere the fragrance of the knowledge of him. For we are to God the aroma of Christ among those who are being saved and those who are perishing. To the one we are the smell of death; to the other, the fragrance of life. And who is equal to such a task? Unlike so many, we do not peddle the word of God for profit. On the contrary, in Christ we speak before God with sincerity, like men sent from God" (2 Corinthians 2:14-17).

We smell. To those who trust in Jesus, we are the sweet fragrance of love and life, like a garden on a spring day. But to those who reject our message, we stink like a sewer—we're the stench of death, and they hate us. As Ray took on the aroma of Christ, some of the people at his university thought it smelled as sweet as cologne, but his parents thought he smelled like a broken septic tank. For us, the question is this: How fragrant are we? Do we have a strong smell of life and death, or is our fragrance almost undetectable. The closer we walk with Christ, the more we'll smell like him, and people around us will treat us the same way they treated him. Some will gladly embrace our message and us, some will walk away, and some will want to kill us. It's the way of the cross. That phenomenon happens every day in my life. If people feel guilty about their sins and angry with God, they don't want to be around me. If they feel overwhelmed with burdens and upset because God hasn't bailed them out, they often avoid me. If they feel loved and forgiven, they want to hang out and talk with me.

As we learn to experience the normal Christian life, there are no guarantees of how people will respond. We can't measure our success by other's response. If Jesus had done that he would have felt like a colossal failure as he stood virtually alone at the trials and with only a handful of faithful people at the foot of the cross. Our task isn't to twist arms to force people to trust Jesus. We simply live it out, show the love of God, tell them what Christ has done for us, make the invitation, and let them respond. Don't be offended if people treat you like they treated Jesus. Take it as an honor, because it is.

✧ Read Acts 5:12-42.

✧ What are some reasons why people (even some religious leaders) seem to be jealous and angry with those of us who see God at work in our lives?

✧ Who is someone you know that is especially fragrant with the aroma of Christ? How do people respond to that person?

✧ What's your fragrance? Do you need to make any changes? If so, what are they?

✧ Complete the following prayer: "Jesus, you smell beautiful! I want to smell more like you. Work your fragrance deep into my heart today. I want to…"

DAY EIGHT | **RIGHT ROLES**

> "So the Twelve gathered all the disciples together and said, 'It would not be right for us to neglect the ministry of the word of God in order to wait on tables. Brothers, choose seven men from among you who are known to be full of the Spirit and wisdom. We will turn this responsibility over to them and will give our attention to prayer and the ministry of the word' " (Acts 6:2-4).

When the Spirit of God is powerfully at work, incredible changes occur, and believers complain. Does that sound like a strange sentence? Think about it. This isn't heaven. We're still human. We have the Holy Spirit living in us, but in any group of Christians, there's a wide range of backgrounds, levels of maturity, and needs. In the early church, it was entirely normal for the Spirit to work powerfully in people's lives, and it was normal for some to gripe. That's real life, and we shouldn't expect anything less.

When people complain, however, we don't have to wring our hands in worry and anger. God is willing to impart his wisdom so that we can overcome any temporary obstacle and move forward, but this time, with more insight and strength than ever. At the beginning of chapter six in the Book of Acts, we see again that the Lord was in harvest mode. More and more people were hearing the message of Christ's forgiveness, and were responding in faith. In our day, divisions can occur in churches along the fault lines of race, economic status, background, and almost any other possible cause of conflict. In the early church, thousands of people were coming to Christ from all races and nations, and a division arose between the Greek Jewish believers and the Hebrew Christians. The Greeks felt their widows weren't getting the attention they deserved. When the line was formed to hand out food, somehow they were consistently left out—and they were hot about it!

Up to this point, the twelve apostles had been doing everything: teaching, preaching, handing out food, and managing the administrative details of the growing church. The problem might have come about because they were overloaded with work. Luke doesn't give us the causes, but the apostles' solution might suggest they had been stretched too thin. Their answer wasn't to buckle down and do more. That wasn't going to work. Instead, they planned to multiply the number of servants and distribute particular roles for groups of workers. They announced, "It would not be right for us to neglect the ministry of the word of God in order to wait on tables. Brothers, choose seven men from among you who are known to be full of the Spirit and wisdom. We will turn this responsibility over to them and will give our attention to prayer and the ministry of the word" (Acts 6:2-4).

A few very important management principles shaped the church at that moment. The top leaders realized the church had grown so much that it was too large for them to manage alone. If it continued, they'd have to neglect their true calling in order to wait tables. There's nothing wrong with humble roles of serving. In fact, every disciple needs to begin there. The Twelve had been serving humbly for a long time as the church began, but now it was time for them to turn the administrative load over to others. What were the qualifications of those selected by the group as servants? They were to be "full of faith and the Holy Spirit," not just warm bodies. Additionally, they all had Greek names. Who had been complaining? Greek believers. Now, the apostles had the right people in the right roles at the right time. It was a perfect match. The apostles commissioned the seven men to serve, honoring them, honoring the role they were to play, and making sure everyone knew the role of the most humble servant is a spiritual ministry serving God and man. What was the result? Luke tells us that again, "The word of God spread. The number of disciples in Jerusalem increased rapidly," and don't miss this, "and a large number of priests became obedient to the faith" (Acts 6:7). From this, I draw the conclusion that when more of God's people are functioning in the right roles, the Spirit's power is unleashed in every corner of the church's life, from preaching in the pulpit to wiping noses in the nursery to helping a stranger at the grocery store. People who serve gladly and effectively are beacons of light and life wherever they serve God, and every role is vital to the life of the church.

Sadly, some of us see the church the way we look at a football game. We expect a few people to work hard and sweat while the rest of us are no more than spectators. That's not the model of the church depicted in the New Testament. All of us are called to know, love, and serve God. We may not all have the same spiritual gifts, talents or roles, but every person is vital to the success of this kingdom enterprise. In his letter to the Ephesians, Paul explained that our roles are God's choosing and design: "For we are God's workmanship, created in Christ Jesus to do good works, which God prepared in advance for us to do" (Ephesians 2:10). This verse doesn't just apply to pastors; it's about every believer. All of us have been created and crafted by the hand of God so that we can make a difference in the destinies of men and women around us. Professor and author, Os Guinness has written extensively on the nature of God's calling for all of us. He insists there is no division between the significance of roles. God sovereignly equips us, and he sovereignly places us—if we'll pay attention. There aren't holy places and secular places, spiritual times and unspiritual times during the day. All believers belong to God all day every day, whether we serve in the pastorate, at home, in offices, in the military, or in school. In his insightful book, The Call, Guinness says that God's design for us is all encompassing. He writes, "God calls us to himself so decisively that everything we are, everything we do, and everything we have is invested with a special devotion and dynamism lived out as a response to his summons and service."

How do we find the right roles in the body of Christ? It's not very different from finding the right vocation. We reflect on what revs our emotional engines. What kind of things stir our hearts, get us excited, create a sense of holy discontent, and cause our creative juices to flow? Quite often, the answer to this question eliminates a lot of options and surfaces others that ring our bells. Then, we dive in and try out a few. We may land on the perfect role from the beginning, but in my experience, that's rare. Far more often, people try a role and they like parts of it, but other aspects don't fit very well, so they try something else. In all of these opportunities, we get input from our spouse, close friends, and ministry leaders to help us discover where we fit best. There's nothing unspiritual in this process at all. It's the way God reveals his wisdom and direction to us. And we may find that our interests change as we grow spiritually or become older. The question for all of us, however, isn't if we serve, but where we serve.

ACT**NORMAL** | RIGHT ROLES

Earlier, we saw that Christ is the head and we can't be unified if we're not all vitally connected to him. In the same way, Paul uses the metaphor of the head and the body to demonstrate the different roles we all play. He wrote to the Corinthians, "The body is a unit, though it is made up of many parts; and though all its parts are many, they form one body. So it is with Christ" (1 Corinthians 12:12).

In an elaborate explanation designed to make the point crystal clear, Paul explains that a human body won't function well if every part is an eye. (Imagine that monstrosity for a minute!) And we're not all ears or noses or mouths, and we're not all feet or kidneys or kneecaps. But how well does a body function without these parts? The simple answer is, not very well. In fact, Paul explains, "Those parts of the body that seem to be weaker are indispensable, and the parts that we think are less honorable we treat with special honor" (1 Corinthians 12:22-23). Every person who serves with a glad heart is performing an honorable function, and there are no first- and second-class servants of God. Paul tells us, "There should be no division in the body, but that its parts should have equal concern for each other. If one part suffers, every part suffers with it; if one part is honored, every part rejoices with it" (1 Corinthians 12:25-26).

Have you ever had an ingrown nail? I have. That little part of my body is a tiny fraction of my body weight, but when it hurts, all my attention is focused there until the pain goes away. When it's functioning well, I don't even think of it. When I go to the hospital or talk to someone on the phone who is sick or injured, I realize how important it is for all the parts of the body to work well together. When I spoke on this passage at The Oaks, some people commented that they didn't want to be nose hairs or intestines or anything so disgusting. I told them, "Hey, I've noticed that some of you are more like butts, and everybody needs a butt! People may not want to get too close to you, but you're important to us."

Every band of believers, from a small group to a mega-church, only functions well when every person finds his or her right fit and performs the tasks with passion for Jesus and the people they serve. To the extent people are on the sidelines, the kingdom misses out on their contributions, and the cause suffers. In four different passages in the New Testament, Paul and Peter outline lists of spiritual gifts, but these lists aren't identical. Why not? I believe these lists are simply representative of a wide range of ways in which people can serve God, just as there are thousands of parts that make up the body, each one being crucial for the body to function well.

I often see people identify their spiritual gifts at the intersection of need and passion. Someone cares deeply about meeting the needs of the indigent in their community, and they do whatever they can to meet that need. Another makes a lot of money, but doesn't use it to buy lavish things for herself. Instead, she delights in secretly helping others in need and contributing to the church's mission. All of us are called to tell our family, friends, and neighbors about Christ, but some of us have a special ability to communicate the gospel. The principle is true for almost all the gifts: we all exercise them to some extent, but a few people have an unusual, God-given ability in teaching, administration, discernment, helping, giving, or some other gift to change lives by the power of the Spirit.

When I find I'm annoyed by some problem, I realize God has put it on my heart. In this case, feeling upset is a sign from the Spirit that he wants me to pitch in to right a wrong or meet a need. Yes, God gives us peace, but he also gives us a heart of compassion, a heart that breaks when we see injustice, poverty, addiction, sin, or anything else that harms the people God loves—and that's everybody. I remember my father being very upset because children couldn't read, but he didn't just sit around and complain. He started a school to help those kids.

Some Christian leaders suggest that spiritual gifts operate only or primarily in the context of the life of a church. I'm not sure where they got that idea. When I look at the life of Christ and the work of the Spirit in the early church, the work of God's people was inside and outside the walls of the building. They lived for Christ all day every day, exercising their God-given talents to make a difference wherever they went. Certainly, greeters and ushers and childcare workers operate in the church during scheduled events, but people who have the ability to make people feel welcome on Sunday morning can use their warmth to build relationships with others everywhere they go. There are no walls in the kingdom of God.

As an organization grows, one of the most important responsibilities of its leaders is to help people connect their passions and gifts with opportunities to serve. It's work, but it's thrilling to help people find the place where they can see God use them to change lives. I love it! Part of my passion is to create organizational structures that help people find the best fit, to equip them to serve effectively, and to celebrate like a maniac when they see lives changed.

Some of you may have been thinking, "I don't know if my 50 hours and $50 will make much of a dent in people's lives. Maybe it's not even worth it." Let me assure you, God is at work in you and through you every time you step out to serve. We may not see dramatic results every time, but two things are sure: God smiles when his children do anything to please him, and he's at work to shape our lives whenever we take steps to help others. He refines our motivations, builds our tenacity, and helps us figure out where we'll fit best next time we serve.

I preached to our church about the roles we play and the motivation of love. After the service, a man, his wife, and their teenage son introduced themselves to me. They had only been attending The Oaks for a few weeks. The man told me, "Pastor, we were at the service last week, and when we got home, several fire trucks were at our house. It had burned to the ground."

I told him, "I'm so sorry. Are you okay?"

"We're more than okay," he smiled. I must have looked surprised, so he continued, "Today you preached on the importance of love, but we didn't need to hear your sermon today. We witnessed that message all week as people from the church poured out their love to our family. My wife and I didn't even know most of these people. They were from my son's small group. They came to our house as soon as they heard what happened, and they helped pull out anything that we could salvage. I don't know where they found the money, but they put us up in a hotel and bought us food all week. I can't tell you what those young people have meant to us."

A few days later, I told this story to our staff, and one of them said, "Pastor Scott, you don't know even half the story."

I almost laughed, "Well, tell me then."

He explained, "Two of the guys who helped at their house that week found out the family needed $10,000 for a down payment on a new home. They came to me and asked what we could do. I could tell the Spirit was working in them, so instead of taking responsibility, I asked, 'What do you think we should do?' They thought for a while, and then they came back with a plan. They decided to look for one hundred people to give $100. And you know what, I think God's going to use them to help that family!"

To find the right role, notice what God has already been doing in your life. Pay attention to what thrills you and annoys you. Where do you already sense God is using you? Where do you find a sense of injustice that propels you to take action? Ask God for direction, and look for open doors. Quite often, God leads us to a structured, existing ministry, but he always brings spontaneous opportunities to care for people around us. Dive in, and watch God use you to change lives. That's normal for people who are part of his body.

✧ **Read Acts 6:1-7.**

✧ **How does a person's role relate to his or her passions, interests, annoyances, and even their view of right and wrong?**

✧ **If you're serving in a role right now, how well do you think you fit there? If you aren't currently serving, what kind of role interests you? Who can you talk to in order to find a good fit?**

✧ **Why do you think the chapter on love (1 Corinthians 13) follows immediately after Paul's description of how the body functions? What's the connection?**

✧ **Complete the following prayer: "Jesus, I'm all yours. I want you to lead me to a place where I can serve most effectively. Today, I'm listening to you for..."**

DAY NINE | CONFIDENCE

> "Now Stephen, a man full of God's grace and power, did great wonders and miraculous signs among the people. Opposition arose, however, from members of the Synagogue of the Freedmen (as it was called)–Jews of Cyrene and Alexandria as well as the provinces of Cilicia and Asia. These men began to argue with Stephen, but they could not stand up against his wisdom or the Spirit by whom he spoke" (Acts 6:8-10).

Stephen had been selected by the people and ordained by the apostles for a task: to serve widows. I can imagine him taking trays of food to little clusters of old ladies, like the Wednesday night dinners some churches have before prayer meeting. I'm sure he smiled and talked to them with all the kindness in the world, but something stirred in him. The gospel was "like fire in his bones," and he found every opportunity to tell people about Jesus. He was happy to serve dinner to widows, but what thrilled his soul was proclaiming the message of Christ.

When Stephen spoke up about Jesus, some people from that part of the Roman Empire began arguing with him. Their problem was that he won the arguments, and they got really hacked off! In their rage, they plotted against him. They convinced some people to say that Stephen had spoken blasphemy (or cursed) Moses and God. Soon, the crowds turned against him. The religious leaders arrested him and brought him in front of the Sanhedrin, the same group Jesus, Peter, and John had faced before. The false witnesses spoke, and then Stephen offered his defense—a detailed story of the faith, from Abraham to Jesus. He wasn't telling them a new story. They had heard and studied the history of the Jewish nation all their lives, but they refused to connect the redemptive story of the Old Testament to the sacrifice of Jesus. Though they said they revered Moses and the prophets, Stephen carefully showed them that everything in the Scriptures pointed to Jesus. Perhaps Stephen had heard the account of the men who walked with Jesus on the road to Emmaus after the resurrection. On that day, "Beginning with Moses and all the prophets, he explained to them what was said in all the Scriptures concerning himself" (Luke 24:27). Stephen was communicating the same broad, powerful message to the Sanhedrin in his trial. He was a student of the Scriptures, and he used it with power and skill.

In John's gospel, we read that Jesus was "full of grace and truth," not one or the other. When people were responsive, Jesus was gentle as a mother, but when they resisted, he spoke plainly about their heart's condition. He called them a "brood of vipers" and "whitewashed tombs." It wasn't delicate language, but he made his point. In the same way, Stephen patiently and persistently narrated the story of God's desire to rescue people from their sins. But when he saw that the religious leaders were rejecting Jesus again, he spoke the plain, hard truth: "You stiff-necked people, with uncircumcised hearts and ears! You are just like your fathers: You always resist the Holy Spirit! Was there ever a prophet your fathers did not persecute? They even killed those who predicted the coming of the Righteous One. And now you have betrayed and murdered him—you who have received the law that was put into effect through angels but have not obeyed it" (Acts 8:51-53).

I'm sure Stephen knew what was coming, and he was ready. The word witness means "martyr," or the willingness to die for a great cause. During the whole process, nothing could shake his faith. Some argued with Stephen, which is to be expected. Others plotted against him and found people to lie about him. "That's terrible," you may say, but that's what they did to Jesus, and "a servant is not above his master." The same religious authorities who condemned Jesus now interrogated Stephen. And when the Sanhedrin refused to listen to the gospel message, they took Stephen outside to kill him, just as they had turned Jesus over to Pilate to be executed. However, even in the face of death, Stephen stayed strong in his faith.

Stephen had a vision of the risen Christ, and the leaders could stand it no longer. Even as he faced the cruel blows of the rocks, he followed the example of Jesus. He prayed, "Lord, do not hold this sin against them" (Acts 8:60). And he died. The men who threw the rocks took off their tunics and gave them to someone to look after while they committed their atrocity against God's choice servant. The man they gave their tunics to was Saul of Tarsus. We'll see him again soon, though we'll know him by his Roman name, Paul. For now, however, he appears for the first time in this drama as an accomplice in the execution of Stephen.

The Spirit gives us confidence to speak up and stand strong through all kinds of difficulties as we try to share the love of God to those around us. And sometimes, we have to move heaven and earth to connect the dots for people. My friend Lee Bramlett is the head of Leadership Development for Wycliffe Bible Translators, an organization that translates the Scriptures into native languages all over the world. It's a fantastic ministry. He spent eight years learning the language of the Hdi people in Cameroon, Central Africa. Only then could he translate the Bible into their language so they could understand the grace of God. The Hdi had no understanding of love and grace. For example, the Hdi believe that sex outside marriage is wrong, but their method of dealing with the problem was to impale the man and woman when the baby was born, letting the blood soak the ground. They never let any crops grow or a house be built on that spot. Here's Lee's story:

It took thousands of years for the Hdi to accept the gift of God's only Son, Jesus Christ. For millennia, they had seen his creation around them. God remained faithful to the Hdi even though generation after generation rejected him. Even so, God was intent on demonstrating his love to them. One of the means God chose to express his unconditional love was in their traditional, unwritten language.

When we went to the remote village of Tourou, there was only one vehicle in town, and it was ours. It took two and a half hours to go eighteen miles over the rugged mountain terrain to reach Hdi land. There was no water or electricity and we used solar power for our computers and printers.

Hdi compounds are composed of multiple huts surrounded by a five-foot high baked mud wall. Even to this day, the Hdi live efficiently and completely off the land. We built round huts, and introduced change to the village when we covered the mud walls with cement and put in cement floors. We each had our own bedroom hut, two beds to a hut. We had an outdoor latrine inside the mud wall perimeter. In the middle of the night, as we made our way to the latrine, we could look up and clearly see the Milky Way. We could see satellites, shooting stars, and planets, as well as an occasional eclipse of the sun or moon. The stars were so bright that we didn't need the kerosene lanterns to make our way around the compound at night.

One of the nicest things about our home in the village was how quiet it got at night. Everyone went to bed around 8:00 p.m. and there was silence—the kind I've only experienced in that village. We enjoyed the complete absence of the hum of electricity and the roar of vehicles. The only sound was the gentle rustle of leaves.

The Hdi language was a spoken language that had never been written. It took me six months to be able to distinguish breaks between words. Though our linguistic training prepared us for the work, it was God who helped us identify the sounds. It's one thing to identify where one thought ends and another begins, but it's another to distinguish the patterns and words in continuous speech. Like most African languages, Hdi is tonal. That is, they distinguish gha (high tone) for mountain and gha (low tone) for a low water wadi. It took over eight years to understand their grammar, but God gave us the resources we needed.

As we were coming to grips with the complexity of the language and culture, we wrote down their rich cultural stories. And as we learned to write it, we had to teach them to read. Each year, we taught five to seven hundred people to read and write their language.

Verbs in English add a suffix to the root word. We add "-ed" to show past tense or "-ing" for present tense. The Hdi language does this also. You can add "-u" or "-a" or "-i," with each one adding a subtle difference to the meaning of the word. For example, "ngh" means to see. If I said, "Ngha the girl," it means, "I saw the girl." "Nghu the girl" means, "I fully see the girl with all my being," or "I lust after the girl." "Nghi the girl" means, "He saw the girl who left."

After a number of years, I had heard and documented two forms of their word for love (dva), but they didn't have a word for the present tense form. One night in a dream, God prompted me to explore the word dvu. The next day, I asked the village leaders, "Can you dvu your wife?"

They laughed, "Of course not!" After a few seconds, one of them explained, "If I said that, I would have to keep loving my wife no matter what she did—even if she never got water for me, or never made me a meal, or committed adultery—why would I keep loving her? No, we'd never say we dvu our wives. We've never heard of such a thing because it doesn't exist."

I asked them, "Could God dvu mankind?" I read John 3:16 in their language, and I changed it to "God so dvu the world that he gave his only begotten Son." There was complete silence for several minutes, and then tears started trickling down the windblown faces of the elders of the village.

One asked, "Do you know what this means? It means that God kept loving us over and over, all these years, while we kept rejecting his love. We have sinned more than anyone, but he still loved us."

My Hdi friends finally comprehended the height, width, depth, and length of God's love and grace. The revelation of God's character in a simple word had been hidden since the beginning of time, but before my eyes, God revealed it to them.

I'm often reminded of Henri Nouwen's insight, "The mystery of ministry is that we have been chosen to make our own limited and very conditional love the gateway for the unlimited and unconditional love of God." It's an honor and a privilege to be part of God's mission to reach people in every part of the world. Firsthand, I saw how God's love has the power to change lives.

Like Stephen and Lee, we can be confident in the God who directs us, the message of hope he has given us, and his love that changes lives. We simply need to make ourselves available, learn a few skills, and find the courage to open our mouths to speak words of hope.

✥ **Read Acts 6:8-8:1.**

✥ **How much preparation do you need to be able to share your testimony of faith in Christ? How will you handle it when people ask questions you can't answer?**

✥ **What factors build our confidence to tell others about Jesus? What factors erode it?**

✥ **Who are two or three people you know who need to hear about the love of Christ? What is your plan for talking with them?**

✥ **Complete the following prayer: "Lord Jesus, your grace changed my life, and I want to make myself available to tell others about you. Today, help me to..."**

DAY TEN | **PAIN WITH A PURPOSE**

> "Those who had been scattered preached the word wherever they went. Philip went down to a city in Samaria and proclaimed the Christ there. When the crowds heard Philip and saw the miraculous signs he did, they all paid close attention to what he said. With shrieks, evil spirits came out of many, and many paralytics and cripples were healed. So there was great joy in that city" (Acts 8:4-8).

Before the moment of liftoff from the hillside, Jesus told his disciples to tell people about him "in Jerusalem, Judea and Samaria, and to the remotest parts of the earth." So far in our story, the believers had remained in Jerusalem. When Stephen was killed, however, the authorities instituted a wave of persecution that caused many Christians to flee for their lives. The letter of James was written to those who were "scattered abroad"—the people who fled Jerusalem and were now refugees in surrounding lands.

God often uses pain as a crowbar to get his children up and moving. I don't know when the disciples would have moved out on their mission trips if God hadn't allowed the persecution to occur. We can't answer that question. All we know is that the fulfillment of the second tier of evangelistic efforts happened when God's people were forced out of their homes because they were going to be captured, imprisoned, and killed. As they ran for their lives, they told everybody they saw about Jesus.

Philip, who was one of the seven deacons commissioned to care for the Greek widows, traveled to Samaria. There, he found a group of people to tell about Jesus, and they responded. These people, Samaritans, we recall from

Jesus' meeting with the woman at the well, were outcasts. The Jews despised them, but God loved them. Philip looked beyond cultural animosities and found love for them. Before long, "there was great joy in that city." Many people trusted in Christ, including a man whose occult powers had amazed many, Simon the Sorcerer.

Later, Peter came down to Samaria to join Philip and help with the awakening. When Simon saw Philip and Peter's spiritual power and popularity, he wanted in on the action. He didn't understand that humility is the source of true power. He offered money to buy the Holy Spirit so he could perform miracles, too. Peter rebuked his faulty concept and his flawed heart, and it appears that Simon was genuinely repentant.

In our culture, our most common question in times of pain isn't, "Lord, how do you want to use this difficulty for your glory?" but "How can I get out of this as quickly as possible?" We're allergic to pain, and in fact, we seem to have a deeply rooted psychological aversion to it. Unfortunately, because we can't stand pain, and think we deserve a life that's free of it, we fail to grasp God's greater purposes for allowing it in our lives. We want to grow close to God and enjoy his blessings, but we don't want to enroll in the school of pain to learn the lessons he can only teach us there.

After Stephen was killed and persecution began, the believers could have panicked. They could have blamed God and bailed on his plan. They could have wondered, "God, what's this all about? I thought you loved us." But we don't read that at all. Certainly, they suffered. They were uprooted from their homes, lost their jobs, and had much of their security taken away, but they used this time of trouble to grow deeper in their faith and reach out to people who had never heard about Jesus. Pain, C. S. Lewis told us, "is God's megaphone" to get our attention, and when he gets our attention, he can teach us valuable principles about what really matters in life.

I've talked to friends who related their experiences of tragic accidents, family illnesses, and other types of calamities, and in those times, God used them to lead a nurse to Christ, comfort a family, or show the love of God to someone who had lost his way. If we're angry or in despair because we're in pain, we'll be completely self-absorbed, and we'll miss open doors—ones God has carefully orchestrated—for us to step into people's lives and give them hope and forgiveness in Christ.

I believe that the sheer volume of information we receive each day has made us emotionally numb. Our hearts simply can't take in all the messages, especially on the 24-hour news cycles that constantly portray images from hurricanes, earthquakes, gang slayings, horrible accidents, and countless other tragedies. A few years ago, Jack Johnson released a song called "The News." The song describes a mother's attempts to shield her child from the brutal realities in the news. She tries to tell her child that the deaths and destruction they see are just make-believe, but she realizes something is missing in the telecast. She asks a piercing question:

"Why don't newscasters cry when they read about the people who die?

You'd think they could be decent enough to put just a tear in their eyes."

As I listened to that song, I realized that I watch the news almost every night, but in many ways, I've become numb to the heartache I see. Like the woman in the song, why don't I have a tear in my eyes? If a friend told me about a loss like one of these, or if I witnessed a horrible event on television, the horror would sink in, and I would probably cry for those who were hurting. But the overload of information from the television news, the radio, and the newspaper is simply too much to absorb. Most of us have disconnected our souls from these painful images, and we are worse off for it.

When my friends and award-winning musicians, Shane Everett and Shane Barnard, recorded their latest album, one of the songs they wrote came from a haunting story from Germany during the dark days of World War II. A church was located near railroad tracks leading to one of the many death camps. One summer during a Sunday worship service, a train carrying Jews to the camp roared by. Men, women, and children had been in the cattle cars for days without sanitation, and the stench from the train was unbearable. Church leaders always kept the doors and windows open in the warm months, so everyone in the building was exposed to the train's awful smell. They may have tried to convince themselves that the train was loaded with dead cattle, but the next week at the same time, the train came by and they could hear the screams of people in the cars. The train must have been going slower because the people in the church heard pitiful pleas for food and water, and for someone to take care of their little children. There was no mistake now what was happening.

The elders of the church met after the service to discuss the predicament. Their plan was to station someone at the tracks to look for the approaching train. When it was near, an elaborate and rapid plan would begin: they'd quickly shut all the windows and doors, and the song leader would lead the congregation in a loud hymn hoping it would drown out the disruptive cries of the people passing on the train.

The song Shane and Shane recorded is called "Turn Down the Music." The message is clear: we who claim to know Jesus and have experienced his compassion need to stop distracting ourselves from hearing the cries of others. We can be involved in all kinds of "spiritual" activities, but if those things numb our hearts to those around us, we'll fail to be the people God wants us to be. Jesus warned against distractions, excuses, and preoccupation when he explained that the two great commandments are to love God and love our neighbors. When someone asked him, "Who is my neighbor?" Jesus told the story of the Good Samaritan. Ironically, the religious people in the story refused to step into the victim's pain and offer aid, but a hated Samaritan was willing to overlook all the cultural prohibitions to care for the wounded man. Who are you? Who am I? Are we like the people in the German church who close our eyes, noses, and ears to the desperate needs of people around us? Are we like the religious leaders in Jesus' story who found convenient excuses for neglecting the needs of a wounded brother? Or will we turn down the distractions, turn up our compassion, and step into the lives of the lost, the hurting, the needy, the smelly, and everyone else in need of our kindness?

After Stephen was killed, Christians were forced to run for their lives. The pain of being uprooted from their comfortable, familiar surroundings, though, was part of God's plan to fulfill the Great Commission by manifesting the Great Commandment's love in them. God is more interested in advancing his kingdom than in the comfort of his children. Am I? Are you? When we experience pain, we can either become hard or soft, bitter or compassionate. It is, I believe, a choice each of us can make. God uses pain to soften our hearts and make them sensitive to the hurts of others, so we'll listen to the cries for help and do whatever it takes to be Good Samaritans for those around us each day.

Though we may not want to experience it—and there are preachers who promise it's not for true believers—pain is normal in our lives. We may try to escape it, mask it, or pretend it's not there, but when we are dishonest about the pain, we don't allow God to produce sensitivity and compassion in us. Make it normal to turn the music down, be honest about your pain, experience a new depth of hope, and then open your heart to those around you who are suffering. We know this for sure: God cares about our pain, and he uses our pain to accomplish good things in and through us. As Christ-followers, it's normal for us to accept the pain in our lives as God's tutor, because he uses it as a catalyst for our growth. Likewise, we shouldn't be too quickly alarmed by the pain we see in others' lives, because God often uses it to reveal his love and hope to them. In reality, pain is normal in the life of the believer. How we choose to address that pain can make all the difference.

✞ **Read Acts 8:1-25.**

✞ **What are some ways people (maybe even you) crank up the music of distractions to avoid feeling the pain of others?**

✞ **What are some reasons we avoid pain in our lives at all cost? What price do we pay in our relationship with God and others for turning up the music?**

✞ **As you've been reading today, who are some hurting people who have come to mind? How can you be a Good Samaritan to them?**

✞ **Complete the following prayer: "Lord, you weren't distracted. You stepped out of heaven and into my life to give me comfort, forgiveness, and strength. Today I want to turn down the music and be more sensitive to…"**

DAY ELEVEN
START WHERE THEY ARE

"Then Philip ran up to the chariot and heard the man reading Isaiah the prophet. 'Do you understand what you are reading?' Philip asked. 'How can I,' he said, 'unless someone explains it to me?' So he invited Philip to come up and sit with him. The eunuch asked Philip, 'Tell me, please, who is the prophet talking about, himself or someone else?' Then Philip began with that very passage of Scripture and told him the good news about Jesus" (Acts 8:30-31, 34-35).

I love Philip. He was willing to serve widows their Wednesday night chicken dinner, but he also longed to tell people about Jesus—and he didn't care who they were. Regardless whether they were the down-and-out or the up-and-coming, he told them all about the love of Christ. Yesterday we saw him reaching out to Samaritans, a people the Jews despised, but today we see him opening his heart to a man who was so powerful and imposing that most of us wouldn't think of approaching him.

While Philip was reaping a harvest of new believers in Samaria, an angel told him to travel fifty miles to a desert road leading from Jerusalem to Gaza. On his way, he met an impressive man, an Ethiopian eunuch who served as the Treasury Secretary for Queen Candace. I can imagine the majestic black man in a fine robe, with all the trappings on his chariot of a wealthy, powerful state official. And I can almost see Philip in a plain tunic, dusty from his walk, and with no observable authority at all. The contrast couldn't have been more pronounced.

The Ethiopian was on his way home from Jerusalem. He was a God-fearing Gentile who wanted to get as close to God as possible. At the temple, he wasn't allowed to go all the way in because he wasn't Jewish. He could only go as far as the Court of the Gentiles. He longed to be close to God, but he was considered an outsider. The Spirit told Philip, "Go to that chariot and stay near it" (Acts 8:29). He didn't tell Philip to preach, to hold a church service, or to do anything weird that would call attention to himself. The Spirit was simply saying, "Be available."

Philip ran up to the chariot and heard the Ethiopian reading a prophecy by Isaiah about the Messiah who would someday come to pay for the sins of the world. With consummate relational skill, Philip simply asked, "Do you understand what you are reading?" (Acts 8:30).

The eunuch replied, "How can I unless someone explains it to me?" He then invited Philip to join him in his chariot. Together, the two men—one who was powerful in the world's eyes, and the other who had the power of the Spirit—read the prophet's prediction that the Lamb of God would be slain for all mankind. The eunuch asked, "Tell me, please, who is the prophet talking about, himself or someone else?"

Talk about an open door! Luke tells us, "Then Philip began with that very passage of Scripture and told him the good news about Jesus" (Acts 8:31-35). The eunuch understood Philip's explanation of the gospel, and he trusted in Jesus. He must have known about the practice of baptism, because after he believed, he asked Philip to immediately baptize him. Can you picture the scene? A powerful, beautifully robed man of the world is dunked under the water by a scruffy guy who simply listened to the Spirit, was open to his leading, and led the first convert in Ethiopia to Jesus. Do you think the eunuch became a light for Christ in his homeland? That's what happened to the woman at the well when she encountered Jesus, and we can easily assume that he also became a flaming evangelist when he arrived back home—a nation that was, by their standards, the uttermost part of the world.

We learn some important lessons from this event. Philip didn't have a strategy to reach Ethiopia for Christ, but God did. Philip wasn't looking for another mission field. He already had plenty of opportunities to tell people in Samaria about Jesus, but he was open to the Spirit's leading. When he saw the Ethiopian in all his splendor, Philip wasn't intimidated. The presence of the Spirit gave Philip confidence to reach out to someone who far outranked him in wealth and political stature. And when the time came to interact with the Ethiopian, Philip didn't arrogantly pronounce the truth. He began the relationship with a question, uncovering the man's heart, engaging his mind, and showing humility and grace to begin to build trust. Philip first looked for how God was already working in the man's life. Only then did he step through the door which the Spirit had already opened.

From this story, I believe there are two primary applications as we learn to live the normal Christian life. First, God wants us to be open to his Spirit so that he can lead us to people who need to know him. I think it can be as simple as when I ask Jenni, my wife, "Where do you want to go out to dinner tonight?" She might say, "For some reason, I'm thinking about the Mexican restaurant where we ate last week. I know we just went there, but I seem drawn there again." And when we're there, God puts us next to someone who needs a word of kindness or perhaps needs to understand the gospel of grace. I'm not saying that God orchestrates every little choice as a piece of the puzzle for world evangelism, but he sometimes leads us to a particular place at a specific time so we can connect with a person whose heart he has prepared. If we're like Philip, open to the Spirit's nudging, we'll have the incredible adventure of being led to men and women who need to know Christ, and we'll have the privilege of telling them the greatest news the world has ever heard. If we're sensitive to the Spirit, we realize we don't have to force anything in sharing Christ with people. We're available, we care deeply, and we look for doors God has already opened. Being led by the Spirit isn't an exact science. Sometimes, I've felt led by God to go to a certain place, but it appeared to be a dry run. I don't know if I missed something or if the other person wasn't obedient to the Spirit's prompting, but nothing happened, at least from my point of view. But there have been far more times when I got into casual conversations that turned into eternally significant ones simply because I realized God had led me to a person, a place, and a time of his choosing. How both of us got there remained a mystery, but when I realized God was at work, I was ready to see God work in and through me to touch someone's life.

The second lesson we can learn from Philip, and one that we've already addressed in other stories in Acts is: don't be strange. Philip didn't use religious language. He didn't pronounce certain words in odd ways to prove he was really religious. He didn't first tell the Ethiopian that he was the answer to his prayers (which, I'm sure, he was). He just stood nearby and asked a simple question. From my observation, Christians often make one of two mistakes in evangelism: they fail to be open to the Spirit out of fear or lack of confidence, or they "bruise the fruit" by being too direct, too religious, or too harsh. Philip provides us with a wonderful example of someone who was open, available, patient, kind, and relevant. Let's follow his model in all our relationships.

Penn Jillette, of the illusionist duo Penn and Teller, posted a video on YouTube to describe an encounter he had with a fan after one of his shows. He says that the man had participated in one of their "Psychic Comedian" sketches, and after the show was over, he approached Jillette. The man told him, "I really liked your show. You're incredibly talented." The man had a Bible in his hand, and he gave it to Jillette, even though he knew Jillette was an atheist. He said, "I want to give you this Bible. I'm a businessman. I'm sane; I'm not crazy." He opened it and showed Jillette where he had written his name, address, five phone numbers, and an email address. "You can contact me anytime in any way you want to," he told him humbly.

On the video, it was obvious that Jillette was deeply touched by the kindness of this fan. He remarked, "If you believe there is a God and you don't tell people, I have no respect for you. If you really believe there is a heaven and a hell and people are going to those places, and you think it's not worth telling people because it would make it socially awkward, that doesn't make sense. How much do you have to hate someone to not tell him? If I believed a truck was bearing down on you, but you didn't believe it, at a certain point, I'd tackle you to get you out of the way. This [eternity] is more important than that. I know there's no God, but [the man who gave me his Bible] is a very, very, very good man. I appreciate that a lot."

Philip was already telling people about Jesus. He had experience in listening to the Spirit, and he had a track record of obeying his whispered instructions. The results were amazing. For you and me, the more we're receptive and obedient to the Lord's nudging, the more we'll become sensitive to opportunities and aware that God is opening doors all around us. As you invest your 50 hours, ask God to lead you, be sensitive to the Spirit, and show kindness as you engage the people who cross your path. Ask questions, be humble, and share the message of Christ from whatever truth or interest the person displays. Hang on. It's going to be lots of fun—and it'll become far more normal than you ever thought it could be!

✤ Read Acts 8:26-40.

✤ What are some ways you can be more sensitive to the Spirit's leading to talk to people about Jesus?

✤ Why are some people weird when they talk about Christ? What does it look like to be normal in these conversations?

✤ How might you start from the Old Testament laws in Deuteronomy, or Leviticus, to explain the gospel to someone? How could you turn a conversation about end times, abortion, or death and difficulties into an explanation of the gospel?

✤ Complete the following prayer: "Father, I want to be more open to you. I ask you to lead me, to make me sensitive to your Spirit's prompting to talk to particular people, and to love them into the faith instead of demanding that they believe. Today, help me to…"

DAY TWELVE | **NEVER GIVE UP**

"Meanwhile, Saul was still breathing out murderous threats against the Lord's disciples. He went to the high priest and asked him for letters to the synagogues in Damascus, so that if he found any there who belonged to the Way, whether men or women, he might take them as prisoners to Jerusalem. As he neared Damascus on his journey, suddenly a light from heaven flashed around him. He fell to the ground and heard a voice say to him, 'Saul, Saul, why do you persecute me?' "
(Acts 9:1-4)

Have you ever given up on someone coming to Christ? Maybe you love this person, but he or she is so threatening, so angry, and so hostile to the faith (and to anyone who would mention Jesus) that you want to stay as far away as possible. Saul of Tarsus was a man like that. He was the Top Gun of Jewish leadership in his day. He had the right family background. He had attended the right schools and had graduated first in his class. He had proven his loyalty to the Jewish faith over and over again, but he wasn't finished. When the new sect of Christ-followers began growing, he dedicated his life to stamping them out. He wasn't going to try to argue them out of existence with his intellect; he used brute force to hunt them down, capture them, bring them to trial, and have them executed. It worked with Stephen, and it would work with all the others. The problem was that the followers of "The Way," as they were called, had skipped town. They ran as far and as fast as they could go. Saul was determined to find them. He headed north to Damascus with his posse to find a few and bring them to justice in Jerusalem.

On the road, however, an amazing event took place. Jesus broke into Saul's life as a blinding light and a voice from heaven. Jesus said, "Saul, Saul, why do you persecute me?" When Jesus said someone's name twice, it was always with quiet compassion. That's a magnificent display of grace. Jesus could have blasted Saul for hurting his people, but instead, he appealed to his heart. His question, though, wasn't "Why are you persecuting the church?" but "Why do you persecute me?" It was personal. Believers are part of Christ's body, so whatever is done to us, is done to him.

Saul's instant response is a question: "Who are you, Lord?" In his culture, a voice from heaven was assumed to be God's own voice, but Saul was confused. He fully believed he was doing God's will. Why in the world would God correct him?

The reply from heaven was, "I am Jesus, whom you are persecuting" (Acts 9:5). Jesus didn't explain the gospel to him the way he had taught the men on the road to Emmaus or at any of his resurrection appearances. For the moment, he made enough of an impression on Saul by blinding him with light and speaking from heaven. And besides, Saul had heard the gospel presented in its entirety by Stephen before he was killed. Saul, as you remember, was the coat rack for the men who threw the stones that day. For now, Jesus gave Saul only one instruction: "Now get up and go into the city, and you will be told what you must do."

My favorite part of this story, and the one that applies to you and me most directly, is what happened when Paul entered Damascus. Three days after Paul arrived, Jesus appeared to a man named Ananias. (This isn't the same guy who died a few chapters ago. Ananias was a very common name in those days.) God told Ananias, "Go to the house of Judas on Straight Street and ask for a man from Tarsus named Saul, for he is praying. In a vision he has seen a man named Ananias come and place his hands on him to restore his sight" (Acts 9:11-12).

I can almost see Ananias' jaw drop as he listened to Jesus. He probably wanted to say, "You gotta be kidding!" but instead he replied with a little more respect. Still, he reminded the Lord of Saul's reputation, "I have heard many reports about this man and all the harm he has done to your saints in Jerusalem. And he has come here with authority from the chief priests to arrest all who call on your name" (Acts 9:13-14).

Jesus reassured him that Saul was now his "chosen instrument to carry my name before the Gentiles," and to make sure Ananias knew Saul wasn't going to get a free ride, he told him, "I will show him how much he must suffer for my name" (Acts 9:16).

In an astounding act of courage, Ananias pushed his very reasonable fears aside and obeyed Jesus. He went to the house where Saul was staying, placed his (probably trembling) hands on the murderer, and prayed for him. Immediately, scales fell from Saul's eyes. Paul got up, was baptized, and got something to eat.

When we think someone is beyond hope and outside the possibility of being transformed by Christ's love, we need to think of Paul. Sometimes the person we've given up on is ourselves. A friend told me about a woman he knows who had to go to a gynecologist. She was a new patient. When she met the doctor, she was terribly ashamed because she had an abortion almost twenty years before. It had haunted her since that day, and she was dying under crushing grief. After only a few sentences passed between them, she began to weep uncontrollably. He guessed the cause because he'd seen this kind of broken heart before. She told him her story, and he asked, "Can't you forgive yourself?"

She shook her head. He then asked bluntly, but with a tone of great kindness, "Do you think you're better than Jesus Christ?"

She looked surprised and answered, "No, not at all."

He smiled, "He forgives you, and if he's willing to forgive you, you can forgive yourself. It's the only way to be free from your guilt and shame."

Later she said, "That was the turning point of my life. From that moment, I was able to accept Christ's forgiveness for the wrong I had done, and because of him, I was able to finally, finally, forgive myself. I never saw that doctor again, but God used him in an incredible way in my life."

Let me share another story of a hopeless person finding hope. In 1940, a twenty-five year old man sat at the corner of Main and Akard Streets in Dallas. He was depressed, grief stricken, and lost. He had nowhere to turn and no idea what to do. He and his young wife had had two small children, but the joys of their life turned to sorrow when both children became ill and died. Later, their third child, Linda Faye, was two and showing signs of serious illness. In addition to their emotional pain, the couple struggled financially. He worked as a truck driver for Phillips Hardware during the day and as a bouncer in his mother's beer joint at night.

Their marriage suffered under all the pressure they were experiencing, and he simply couldn't stand it any longer. He began drinking to numb the pain. As he sat on the side of the road one night, this young man made a decision that changed not only the course of his life, but mine as well. He cried out, "God, I don't know anything about you. I don't know how to pray, and I've never owned a Bible, but if you'll show me how to find you, I'll give my life to you."

Later that night as he was walking down the street, he heard singing coming from a little storefront. It was a revival meeting. He didn't go in, but he stood outside the door listening for an hour or so. The next night, he went back and stood outside the service again. On the third night, he decided he was going to go in and sit on the back row. He wanted to hear clearly what the preacher was saying. That night, my papaw heard the plan of salvation for the first time. He later remembered, "It was the greatest feeling in the world to go down to the altar and give my life to Jesus. A ton of bricks lifted off me. It changed everything inside me and I knew I'd never be the same."

He bought a guitar and taught himself two gospel songs. Two days later, he was on a street corner singing those songs and telling anyone who would listen about the love and forgiveness he had found in Christ. From then on, my papaw made it his life's goal to bring as many people to Christ as he could. His perspective was clear, powerful, and simple: "If Jesus Christ can change me, he can change anybody. No one is beyond the hope of the gospel." He kept spreading that message until the day he died. He was one of the most passionate witnesses I have ever known and one of the greatest heroes in my life. The decision my papaw made that night on the corner of Main and Akard changed not only the course of his life, but the lives of countless others. Because of his decision to trust Christ instead of giving up in despair, my mother grew up in a Christian home, I grew up in a Christian home, and my kids are growing up in a Christian home—all because a twenty-five year old alcoholic said "Yes" to Jesus.

My papaw never forgot how far Christ had brought him—from shame to hope, from despair to joy, from sin to forgiveness, from emptiness to purpose. People who met him the day before he trusted Jesus might have shaken their heads and thought, "There's no hope for that guy." But they don't know the power of God to bring light into a dark heart. When Paul was an old man, he told Timothy that he was "the chief of sinners." That assessment wasn't a source of shame, but of deep humility. Because Jesus changed a kidnapper and murderer into a saint, Paul was convinced that every person he met was within the circle of God's grace—if they'd only take his outstretched hand.

It's normal for God's love and power to reach into sin-darkened hearts, but it's also normal for him to ask the Ananiases of the world—people like you and me—to be willing to show love and kindness to anyone who has let the light of Christ shine on them—gang members and prostitutes, powerful officials and homeless people, the fabulously wealthy and the pitifully poor, people of our race and people who are of different languages and skin colors.

We label people as if it's the final word on their character. We call them liars, criminals, addicts, abusers, selfish, cruel, shallow, and a hundred other names, and if we're honest, many of us use those same kind of labels about ourselves in the privacy of our secret thoughts. But God is willing to change our labels. If he could change Saul from a murderer into a choice servant, he can change anybody. That's the business he's in—it's normal for him.

Is there anyone in your life that you've given up on?

✥ **Read Acts 9:1-19.**

✥ **Who are the people you know who seem most antagonistic or apathetic to Christ? What does the story of Paul's conversion say to you about those people?**

✥ **Are there any believers who make you feel uncomfortable or threatened? How can you be like Ananias to them?**

✥ **How does remembering our own stories of initially meeting Christ give us compassion for those who are still outside the faith?**

✥ **Complete the following prayer: "Lord Jesus, you're willing to touch anybody with your grace, even me. Use me to reach out to people who are different, threatening, and repulsive. Today, I will..."**

DAY THIRTEEN | ENCOURAGEMENT

"When he came to Jerusalem, he tried to join the disciples, but they were all afraid of him, not believing that he really was a disciple. But Barnabas took him and brought him to the apostles. He told them how Saul on his journey had seen the Lord and that the Lord had spoken to him, and how in Damascus he had preached fearlessly in the name of Jesus" (Acts 9:26-27).

Luke's account of the first weeks of Saul's life with Christ reads like the Bourne trilogy, full of intrigue, chases, and escapes. In that day, like this one, conspiracies were rampant. People changed allegiances, or pretended to change in order to trick their adversaries. The Christians of that day had fled Jerusalem because a vicious man was hunting them down. Saul might be compared to Heinrich Himmler, the Nazi Gestapo henchman who orchestrated the Final Solution to exterminate the Jews. People were terrified at the mention of his name. Now, in Damascus, Paul walked into the local synagogues to speak. The people sitting there expected him to spew out venom about the new sect of Christians, but to their shock, he announced that Jesus was the Son of God. Luke tells us, "All those who heard him were astonished and asked, 'Isn't he the man who raised havoc in Jerusalem among those who call on this name? And hasn't he come here to take them as prisoners to the chief priests?'" (Acts 9:21)

Dramatically, the tables turned. As Paul spoke powerfully about Christ, the Jewish leaders, his former allies, hatched a plot to kill him. Paul, however, discovered their plan and late at night it was the Christians, who had run from him only a few days before, who lowered him over a wall in a basket.

He escaped to Jerusalem, and the few remaining believers in the city were extremely suspicious. They wondered if he was infiltrating their ranks to discover the identities of the Christians so he could capture them and turn them over for trial. At that critical moment, Paul was a man without a country. The Jewish authorities wanted to kill him because he had turned on them, but the Christians didn't believe his conversion story was real. Through the fog stepped a man who embraced the renegade and changed the course of the church. Barnabas, the trusted, respected man who had proven his loyalty by giving all he had to provide for the needs of others, brought Paul to the church leaders and defended his story.

With the fresh blessing of the church leaders, Paul began speaking out about Jesus in Jerusalem. Again, the Jews plotted to kill him, but the Christians discovered the plan and took him to the coastal city of Caesarea and later to his hometown of Tarsus. The chief threat to the stability of the church had been neutralized by the grace of God, and God gave the believers a time of peace and harvest as countless more came to faith. Soon, we'll see a dynamic duo composed of Saul, soon to be called Paul, and Barnabas as they take the message of Christ to the whole Roman world. This was, perhaps, the most important partnership in the history of God's work in the world.

Barnabas exemplified three traits that are essential for anyone desiring to be a powerful instrument of encouragement: discernment, courage, and availability. All of us know people who have sunny dispositions. I love to be around optimistic people as they bring joy to almost any situation. Some of these people, however, aren't the most discerning and astute people on the planet. Barnabas was optimistic about Paul, but even more, he had piercing discernment to see through the situation in order to separate truth from fiction and reality from conspiracy. Accusations were flying, and even some mature believers had developed strong opinions about Paul's claim to be a new believer. Perhaps Barnabas had learned to read people having being involved in business deals in the past, maybe he was a naturally perceptive person like many counselors I know, or perhaps God gave him a spiritual capacity of discernment when he became a believer. Luke doesn't tell us how he became shrewd, only that he had sharp insight into Paul's heart to see that his faith was genuine when others had every reason in the world to doubt it. His support of Paul wasn't blind optimism. God gave him spiritual insight about a man, his story, and the potential of this man to revolutionize the world.

Not everyone who talks about God is someone we need to get behind. Certainly, we don't want to be negative and judgmental people, but there's a difference between being discerning and judgmental. A discerning person's heart breaks when they see someone whose heart isn't right before God yet wears a mask of spirituality. A judgmental person may see the same problems, but he delights in finding and exposing the faults of others.

It's hard to say "Yes" when everyone else is saying "No." It's hard enough to "go against the flow" when it comes to the everyday decisions in life, but how much more difficult would it be to defend the veracity of a man when being wrong might mean death for hundreds of people, including family and friends? It would have been much easier for Barnabas to go with the flow and let the doubters have their way with Paul. Their position was certainly reasonable—who could deny the fact that this man had been their most ruthless enemy only a short time before? But Barnabas found the courage to stand up for a man he, as far as we know, had never met and only known by reputation. Still, he displayed the courage of his convictions to speak out boldly for Paul.

It wasn't enough, though, for Barnabas to make a pronouncement about Paul and then back away from him. His affirmation came with a large blob of glue—the two men became fast friends, compatriots, and partners in taking the gospel to Asia and Europe. Barnabas was available to God to teach the greatest teacher the church has ever known and shepherd the man who wrote the book on spiritual leadership. To have this kind of impact, he had to be there day after day and year after year. Everything Paul accomplished for God had the fingerprints of Barnabas on it.

Actress Celeste Holm once commented, "We live by encouragement and die without it—slowly, sadly, angrily." Encouragement has astonishing power to give life and breathe hope into a person's life. A few words of affirmation can make a world of difference. Author and pastor Robert Lewis says every child—and I'd expand it to every spouse, parent, and friend—needs to hear three messages: "I love you," "I'm proud of you," and "You're good at this or that skill." These may seem like simple words, but if they're spoken sincerely, they bring hope to a troubled heart and encourage successful people to excel even more. A friend of mine got a note from a man expressing his heartfelt appreciation. It was specific and warm. My friend commented, "I'll live on that note of encouragement for a week or two!"

It's not good enough to encourage the sweet people and the ones who make us feel good. Jesus said that's not much of a measure of love. We show his love when we care for those who can't give anything back to us, the ones who are rough around the edges, the people no one else wants to connect with, the hurting, the defensive, those who still curse a lot, and those who smell bad. In many cases, we have to look beyond the obvious deficiencies of others and their past reputations, but like Barnabas, we can find something good about them and speak words of faith, hope, and love. When we walk into a church service, who do we sit next to? Most of us find someone we know and like, but maybe we should look for someone who looks uncomfortable or out of place. Who do you gravitate to at a party? Most of us hang out with our best friends, but maybe we should look for those who are alone. We don't have to be silly about this. It's not wrong to want to be with friends, but sometimes, at least every now and then, we need to look for people who could use a kind word and a smile.

My brother-in-law, Mark, pastors a church in Mesquite, Texas. Two men who had been convicts were saved and came to the church, and they found such love and encouragement there that they began inviting other ex-cons. In only three months, over fifty people had joined the church, and forty-five of them were ex-cons. Do you think they felt threatened and unwelcome at other places? Of course they would. Can you imagine they had their antennae up to see if anyone would really love and accept them? You bet. Mark has been meeting with many of these people, and he gloriously accepts them as they are. They've been looking, hoping, longing for someone to show them genuine love, and they found it in Mark and his church.

Sometimes, the person who needs encouragement isn't a criminal or a rebellious, angry person, but a wounded one. Annie, a young woman in our community, became disillusioned with her parents, the church, and God. She came to the conclusion that people who had anything to do with God were fakes, and she wanted no part of them. She started spending time with a young man who had no interest in God. After a few weeks, he raped her, and she became pregnant. Annie was devastated. She carried the child to birth and put it up for adoption. At that moment, she felt that she was the scum of the earth. She was disconnected from her family, from God, and from any sense of safety and security. Rachel, a young woman who attends the Gathering, our young adults' ministry, befriended Annie. Gradually, this troubled young woman began to trust again. After several months, the two became fast friends, and God began to work in Annie's life. She came back to Christ, experienced forgiveness she had never known before, and found a new place to call her spiritual home. All of this happened because Rachel was willing to reach out to connect with someone who seemed disinterested, and in fact, fiercely opposed to anyone or anything representing God. Later, I talked to Annie's father. He told me, "Scott, I've never seen anything so miraculous as the change in my daughter's life. I'm so grateful for the young lady in your church who cared enough to look past her resistance and really love her."

Quite often, the people who need those words and smiles live under our roofs. It's easy to take our families for granted, and little annoyances can grow into major divisions. If we're not careful, we can become harsh, critical, and focused only on what they do wrong instead of what they do right. One mother heard me talk about the importance of encouraging kids, and she reacted angrily, "I don't know what you're talking about. My son never does anything right!" God has given us the privilege and responsibility to shine the light of his love into the lives of those closest to us, and everyone else as well. All of us—especially parents of toddlers and teenagers—need to overlook as many annoying behaviors as we can and make a point to find something positive each day (yes, every day) to notice, name, and nurture.

I want to be like Barnabas, known for the ability to encourage people. It's normal to be annoyed, but if the Spirit is transforming our hearts, it becomes normal to love the unlovely.

✤ **Read Acts 9:20-31.**

✤ **What's the difference between discernment and being judgmental, and between discernment and blind optimism?**

✤ **Who is the most encouraging person you know? What kind of impact does that person have on others?**

✤ **Why is it important to be sincere, specific, and persistent when we encourage people?**

✤ **Complete the following prayer: "Lord, I want to be more like Barnabas, shrewd and encouraging. Today, I want to speak words of hope to…"**

DAY FOURTEEN | **NO LIMITS**

> "Then Peter began to speak: 'I now realize how true it is that God does not show favoritism but accepts men from every nation who fear him and do what is right. All the prophets testify about him that everyone who believes in him receives forgiveness of sins through his name' "
> (Acts 10:34-35, 43).

God's design to reach every person on earth with the gospel wasn't new when Jesus gave the disciples the Great Commission. That was his plan all along. When God commissioned Abraham, he promised, "All peoples on earth will be blessed through you" (Genesis 12:3). Several of David's psalms explain God's desire to reach all nations. The writer of Chronicles records, "Give thanks to the Lord, call on his name; make known among the nations what he has done" (1 Chronicles 16:8). In a clearly Messianic psalm, David writes, "All the ends of the earth will remember and turn to the Lord, and all the families of the nations will bow down before him" (Psalm 22:27). Isaiah, Ezekiel, Daniel, Jonah, and other prophets remind the beleaguered nation that God's grand plan doesn't just include restoring the nation of Israel, but restoring every person on the planet to a right relationship with him.

The Jewish people, however, didn't seem to understand. Even Jesus' disciples had a hard time grasping the broad sweep of God's purposes. Their cultural roots trumped Christ's example of reaching out to everyone by hating the Samaritans and annoying the Greeks. At this moment in Luke's narrative, we see that the gospel of grace knows no limits. As we follow Christ, we have to follow his agenda instead of insisting that he follow ours.

A Roman officer named Cornelius lived in the seacoast town of Caesarea. He and his family loved God, gave to the local synagogue, and devoted themselves to prayer. One afternoon Cornelius had a vision of an angel who instructed him to send for Peter, who was staying in Joppa, a town just up the coast. Cornelius gave instructions to two of his servants and a soldier to find the fisherman.

At noon the next day, Peter went up to the roof of the house to pray. While lunch was being prepared he became hungry and fell into a trance. He saw a huge sheet come down from heaven containing all kinds of animals, including those that Jews were not allowed to eat. Then a voice spoke, "Get up, Peter. Kill and eat" (Acts 10:13).

Peter had lived according to Jewish dietary laws his whole life. Their customs defined them as a nation and each individual as a devout believer. Peter's instant response was revulsion. He responded, "Surely not, Lord! I have never eaten anything impure or unclean" (Acts 10:14).

The voice explained, "Do not call anything impure that God has made clean" (Acts 10:15).

While Peter was in the trance on the roof, the sheet appeared and the voice spoke three times. Peter was perplexed, but at that moment, three men knocked at the door. They announced that they were looking for Peter, and the Spirit told him, "Simon, three men are looking for you. So get up and go downstairs. Do not hesitate to go with them, for I have sent them" (Acts 10:19-20).

The men explained why they had come. They told Peter about Cornelius's faith in God and the vision he had seen. The next day, Peter left Joppa with the three men. When he arrived in Caesarea and heard Cornelius's story, he realized the significance of the vision he had seen. He told Cornelius, his family, and all those who were in the room, "I now realize how true it is that God does not show favoritism but accepts men from every nation who fear him and do what is right" (Acts 10:34-35). Finally, Peter understood what the Great Commission really meant. He explained the gospel to them, and was astonished when the Holy Spirit came upon all of them. Even Gentiles were of equal standing in God's family! Peter baptized them, and stayed with his new family members for a few days.

What are the limits of grace in our hearts? Who are the people we exclude without even thinking twice about it? For Peter, the idea of reaching out to Gentiles wasn't even on his radar, but it was certainly on God's. A few years ago (and maybe in a few corners of the church today), a large number of believers were scornful of anyone who drank, danced, went to movies, wore make-up, or played golf on Sunday. Those judgments have been relaxed in most communities, but we still tend to accept people who are like us and shy away from—if not reject—people who are different. We may not clearly articulate our preferences and prejudices, but we have second thoughts about people when we see them smoking, if their skin color is different, if their language sounds odd, if their style of worship seems foreign, if they drive up in a beat up old car, if they've been divorced several times, or countless other things we can use as dividers in our hearts.

Like many of us, Peter had a natural distaste or suspicion of those who were different from himself, especially when these differences were significant and culturally ingrained. God called Peter to tear down those walls and reach across the boundaries to show genuine love. He wants us to tear down the walls in our lives as well. In the weeks after General Robert E. Lee surrendered to General Ulysses S. Grant at the Appomattox Court House, people on both sides were exhausted and bitter. Lee had come back to Richmond to live with his invalid wife Mary. One Sunday at church, the pastor held communion and asked people to come to the altar to receive the elements and pray. A black man got up, walked to the front of the packed church, and knelt at the altar. A tense quiet permeated the room. No black person had ever attended the church before, and certainly hadn't received communion along with the white people. No one knew what to do. The pastor stopped the service and stood silent. After a few awkward seconds, an old man slowly got up and walked alone to the front of the church. He knelt next to the black man and bowed his head in prayer. It was General Lee. The man who had led the South's finest army was the most revered man in the nation. In his humility and grace, he created an atmosphere for reconciliation in the most powerful way possible—in church, during Holy Communion, kneeling next to a man who had been a slave only weeks before.

I'm not sure what General Lee was thinking at that moment, but he read the Scriptures every day. Perhaps he was reflecting on Paul's statement in his letter to the Galatians: "You are all sons of God through faith in Christ Jesus, for all of you who were baptized into Christ have clothed yourselves with Christ. There is neither Jew nor Greek, slave nor free, male nor female, for you are all one in Christ Jesus. If you belong to Christ, then you are Abraham's seed, and heirs according to the promise" (Galatians 3:26-29).

Young Life is a dynamic ministry to high school students across the country. Their purpose isn't to compete with the church, but to be the voice of grace to students who would never attend church. They delight when students who are smoking outside, high from drugs, or have slept with their girlfriend or boyfriend come to their meetings. "Those are the people God wants us to reach," one staff member said. But in almost every community, there are Christians who don't understand. Parents and church leaders criticize the Young Life staff and volunteers for letting such "rough kids" come to their meetings. One mother remarked with obvious anger, "I wouldn't let my daughter go to a meeting where those people are welcome!"

The staff member replied calmly. "That's fine, but those are exactly the people God wants us to love into his kingdom."

That's the attitude of our church, too. I'm thrilled when I see cigarette butts in the parking lot after a service or hear that someone came who was so hung over that he could barely walk. In some churches, people are appalled when "unclean" people come for worship or join a small group, but God has given our people warm and open hearts. We delight when they come. A friend told me that a man in his church had just come to Christ. His first act was to throw away all his cheap whiskey and buy only the best. He explained, "My body is the temple of the Holy Spirit, and I need to put only good stuff in it!" My friend didn't jump down his throat. He saw this man's choice as the first step in following Christ, with many more to come.

During the campaigns for local elections, we often invite people running for judge to come to our church so we can pray for them. Not long ago, I explained to our congregation that several of our pastors know the incumbent judges very well because they've gone to court to support people from The Oaks who are in trouble. Some people thought I was joking, but I told them that I was proud to be the pastor of a church that had ex-cons in it. Paul wrote to the Corinthian church to instruct them how to handle all kinds of sticky legal and relational problems. Our church—and every other church in the world that's reaching the lost—is no different. If a group of believers is content to have just a "holy huddle" and exclude people who smoke, drink, gamble, commit adultery, harbor bitterness, talk funny, or wear old clothes, they can keep their carpets clean and eliminate some hassles, but they won't be the people God has called them to be. From Genesis to Revelation, we see that God turned things upside down. Those who thought they were insiders and had it all together became outsiders in the kingdom of grace, but every person, no matter how dirty or sinful, who trusted in Jesus for forgiveness, became a gloriously accepted and loved child of God in the faith.

When we see Peter in this part of Luke's story, we don't see a man with a hard heart. Jesus had restored him after his denials. On the day of Pentecost, he was the chief spokesman for God, and three thousand people were saved. God used him to heal a crippled man, to stand up to the Sanhedrin, and to keep leading people to Christ during this time. But this Spirit-filled, Spirit-directed, Spirit-empowered man of God still had some things to learn about God's purposes. He was under the impression that only Jews could be Christians, and God had to orchestrate a vision for a Gentile and a repetitive vision for Peter to help him break out of his cultural box. Only then did Peter reach out and embrace a man, his family, his associates, and an entire race of people God loved.

I wonder about you, but even more, I wonder about me. How much do we live by our cultural mandates instead of opening our arms to every person God loves. We may not have the same rigid, negative, entrenched perspective that Jews had about Gentiles, but maybe we subtly shy away from certain types of people. One of the lessons in this passage is that no matter how much we know about God, and no matter how faithfully we serve him, we still have a lot to learn about God's will and his ways. The Lord didn't blast Peter and condemn him for not understanding the scope of the Great Commission. He gently and clearly showed him what he wanted him to do. God often uses books, CDs, talks with friends, talks at conferences, and most importantly, the Scriptures to challenge my thinking to get me out of my culture-constructed boxes. I'm not surprised when the Spirit nudges me and says, "Hey Scott, you kind of avoided that person. What's that about? Any change needed?" Any avoidance or judgmental spirit shows me that I still have something to learn.

If God sent you a vision today, what would it say to you? If people outside your box knocked on your door today, who might they be? Think, pray, and be open to God. The process of learning to widen our boundaries is a normal part of life for anyone who is serious about following Jesus—people like you and me.

✧ **Read Acts 10.**

✧ **Why do you think it took a vision and a knock on his door for Peter to understand something about God's design that he had heard his whole life from many different passages of Scripture and from Jesus himself?**

✧ **What kinds of people annoy you? What kinds arouse a critical spirit? What do these responses show you?**

✧ **Who has the Lord put on your heart as you read today's lesson? How will you reach out to that person, or those people?**

✧ **Complete the following prayer: "Jesus, you reached out to everybody, and you weren't turned off by their sins or their stench. Today, show me who is knocking on my door..."**

DAY FIFTEEN | **WILLING TO CHANGE**

"The apostles and the brothers throughout Judea heard that the Gentiles also had received the word of God. So when Peter went up to Jerusalem, the circumcised believers criticized him and said, 'You went into the house of uncircumcised men and ate with them' " (Acts 11:1-3).

It's one thing for an individual to reach out to people who are different, but it's quite another for a whole congregation to break out of a rut. When Peter went back to Jerusalem after seeing the Holy Spirit poured out on Cornelius's household, he caught flack from people who were as narrow minded as he had been only a few days before. The Jewish Christians basically said, "I can't believe you went to their house, and oh my gosh, you ate with them! What in the world were you thinking?" The problem was that in their culture, eating with someone showed complete acceptance and equality. Like Peter, before he saw the visions of the sheet, these Christians were completely convinced that God's grace stopped at the door of the Gentiles. Prejudice isn't just seen in individuals; it's perpetuated and reinforced in organizations that communicate, "We're right and you're wrong," or "We're in and you're out."

I don't think Peter was very surprised at their reaction to the news. He would have been in their shoes if God hadn't worked a miracle in his own heart. Luke tells us, "Peter began and explained everything to them precisely as it had happened" (Acts 11:4). He carefully explained every part of the story. He wanted to put them "in the moment" so they could feel what he felt and learn what he learned about how God had expanded his perception of the kingdom. After listening to the entire story, especially the part about the Holy Spirit being poured out on them, they were finally convinced. Luke says, "When they heard this, they had no further objections and praised God, saying, 'So then, God has granted even the Gentiles repentance unto life' " (Acts 11:18). This was an important moment in establishing the church as many nations in one body, but it wouldn't be the last time Christians objected to the inclusion of people who were different—in the first century and today.

In his book, Who Stole My Church?: What to Do When the Church You Love Tries to Enter the 21st Century, author and pastor Gordon McDonald describes the current crisis in the church as older believers try to cope with new worship styles, technology, language, and the culture of young believers. McDonald describes the price we have to pay for inclusion, a price some of us are very reluctant to pay. Peter had to pay the price of ridicule and suspicion for his obedience to the Spirit and his acceptance of Gentiles into the family of God. Jesus paid with his life for inverting the accepted norms, accepting prostitutes, tax gatherers, sick people and women over the objections of the religious establishment. In every culture and in every body of believers, we face the challenge of grace-filled inclusion. We have to determine where we draw the lines—and certainly, there are boundaries we must draw around the deity of Christ, the authority of Scripture, the work of the Spirit, forgiveness from the cross, and new life from the resurrection—but we must be careful not to draw lines where Jesus didn't draw them. When we exclude people because of race, ethnicity, background, or any other cultural reason, we cloud the gospel in people's minds.

As McDonald describes in his book, many of the conflicts in churches today aren't about theology and purpose; they're about the style of worship and the direction of ministry. Jack Mourning is a wonderful man of God in our church. A few years ago, we realized we needed to add another service on Sunday mornings to welcome more people who want to know Christ. To make it work, we had to shorten all our services, which cut down on the number of songs we could sing and the length of the message. When we rolled out this plan, Jack came to me and expressed his objections. He told me that he wasn't getting as much out of the service as he used to, but he quickly said, "I'm praying. I'm open to the Lord in this."

As Jack prayed, the Lord gave him confirmation that the new direction was his plan. That was enough for Jack. Like the leaders who heard Peter's explanation of the Holy Spirit's work in Caesarea in the lives of Gentiles, Jack trusted that the Spirit was going to work powerfully through this new direction for our church. I really appreciate the way he handled it. He disagreed and had concerns, but he didn't launch a campaign to undermine the leadership of the church. He didn't gossip, and he didn't complain. He spoke his heart and prayed, and God gave him the answer he needed. At that point, he became a huge fan of the new direction, not because he loved it, but because he loved God.

Later, I asked Jack to join the staff of our church. I told him, "The day you told me you disagreed with a decision but you'd pray about it, I knew I could trust you. And then when you came back and said that God showed you that we were obeying him and you'd be happy to get on board, I was really impressed with your heart. You were willing to do church God's way, not your way. That's so cool."

One of the marks of real spiritual maturity and leadership is a willingness to allow God to shake up our preconceptions. All of us have an idea of how God should work. That's a given. But to grow, we need to be open to God's directions so we can take advantage of new opportunities he gives us. Too often, we spend all our efforts trying to get God to bless our agenda instead of coming to him with a blank piece of paper and asking him to show us his. I'm not talking about theology here; I'm talking about style, direction, and people in our communities. Sometimes, God reveals his agenda and changes our direction when we come face to face with the desperate needs in people's lives.

Many years ago, I was a youth pastor at my father's church. Our ministry was strong and growing, but tragedy threatened to ruin it. Many young people, including some who were part of our youth group, joined gangs. One night, a young man was killed in a drive-by shooting. The horrible incident shook the whole church, and it set the stage for a change of directions for my father and our community of faith. Dad wanted to do something to help kids stay out of gangs and find meaning, so God led him to become the founder of a charter school. My Dad went back to graduate school at the age of 65 to get his Ph.D. in public administration from the University of Texas at Dallas. He put his life and career on the line. He gave up his pastorate to pursue his new calling in education. Mahatma Gandhi said, "You must be the change you wish to see in the world." I'm so glad my Dad was open to the leading of the Spirit in his life because Life School has become a beacon of light in a dark world of hurting and lost kids in our community.

Even though God is always doing something new, his directives are fresh in every culture and community and will always conform to biblical truth. He has proven the depth of his love by Christ paying the ultimate price for us, and he offers his infinite creativity to those who are willing to say, "Lord, not my will but yours, not my agenda but yours, not my cultural boxes but your expansive heart to reach every person—that's what I'm committed to. Lead me, Lord. I'm yours."

A broken heart is a catalyst for change. Do we care more about the eternal destinies of people around us or about our own convenience? Are we more concerned about the reality of heaven and hell than we are about our pleasures? Do we care enough about people that we're willing to change, break down our norms, and create new strategies to reach them? I don't think we should underestimate the passive power of inertia. Peter had been with Jesus for over three years and had seen the Spirit work miracles. He had heard and read the Scriptures about God's desire for people for every nation to know him, but until God shook him out of his lethargy, he remained stuck in a rut. I don't think you and I are much different. We may think we're bold and creative, but most of us probably live in fairly carefully defined boxes of what we think are safe and acceptable.

We live in the most wonderful nation the world has ever known, and we enjoy incredible blessings. If we're not careful, we can begin to expect to experience heaven on earth. When that happens, we lose the cutting edge of our faith. We become self-absorbed, asking God to give us more and more stuff instead of understanding that God blesses us so we can pay it forward to bless others. And if our hope is in the stuff of this world, we lose the urgency of sharing the gospel with others. Do we really believe in a real heaven and a real hell? A woman asked Pastor Tim Keller if he really believed the absurd description of hell as a place of unending fire. Keller replied, "Well, the description of heaven and hell in the Bible are metaphors. It says heaven is 'like' a feast, 'like' pure gold, and 'like' many other things. We can conclude that these terms can't really describe the glory and beauty of heaven because it's more wonderful than words can depict. In the same way, 'fire' is a metaphor for hell. I don't believe in literal fire." The woman looked relieved, but he continued, "Hell is much worse than the word 'fire' can describe. 'Fire' just gives us a metaphor of how bad it will be."

God wants to shake us out of our complacency and stagnant presuppositions. Often the way he does this is by showing us the desperate needs of people, needs the church isn't meeting, and the people Christ died to save. It's normal for God to have to shake us from time to time. When he does, we need to respond like the church's leaders in Jerusalem did. They praised God for expanding their vision of his goodness and glory, and we should also.

✚ **Read Acts 11:1-18.**

✚ **What kind of resistance to change have you seen in churches and other organizations?**

✚ **How does God use others' needs to shake us out of our complacency?**

✚ **How does a deeper grasp of the reality of eternity help you be more willing to accept God's agenda for change?**

✚ **Complete the following prayer: "Jesus, you blew all the boxes apart when you were on earth, and I think you still want to do that today. I'm open, Lord. Yesterday, I looked to see who was knocking at my door. Today, I want to take action to open the door and build a relationship with that person. Help me to…"**

DAY SIXTEEN
STRATEGIC OPPORTUNITIES

> "Now those who had been scattered by the persecution in connection with Stephen traveled as far as Phoenicia, Cyprus and Antioch, telling the message only to Jews. Some of them, however, men from Cyprus and Cyrene, went to Antioch and began to speak to Greeks also, telling them the good news about the Lord Jesus. The Lord's hand was with them, and a great number of people believed and turned to the Lord" (Acts 11:19-21).

How does God accomplish his purposes in the world? Quite often, it's not by protecting his children from pain and struggles, but by exposing them to suffering so their faith can shine like a lighthouse to the people around them. In our culture, we don't suffer well. We whine, we complain, and we want to escape as quickly as possible. We're convinced that the abundant life is all happiness and pleasure, so pain simply can't be part of God's plan. Pain, however, is an essential tool in the life of individual Christians and the church as a whole. When we encounter heartaches, we need to ask, "God, what are you up to? How do you want to use this in my life? How do you want to use this pain to deepen my faith?" Those are the right questions. In the early church, the believers were under no illusions. They were real people living in the real world following a God who was willing to subject them to all kinds of difficulties. For them, enduring through difficult situations demonstrated their real character, like squeezing a sponge—whatever was already there would flow out. When God squeezed them, he found genuine faith.

The persecution that began after the execution of Stephen remained hot and fierce. As Christians traveled away from Jerusalem, they told people about Jesus. There were still a few who didn't get the memo about the Gentiles being part of God's kingdom, but some others understood. Wherever they went, more people believed. When we look at the word "persecution" on a page, it may not have the emotional impact of seeing images, like reading an article about the Holocaust and imagining images of the death camps. The believers—the ones who fled Jerusalem and were telling people wherever they went about Jesus—were political and religious refugees. They suffered the pangs of being uprooted from their homes and having to leave friends and the comfort of their familiar surroundings behind. As they traveled, they had to find shelter and food. Now remember, they were running because the Jewish leaders wanted to kill them. This wasn't like an evacuation from a natural disaster. It was more like a jailbreak! The authorities pursued them. If there had been "Most Wanted" posters in post offices, their pictures would have been on display. Their world was a mess, but they refused to give in to despair. Even in their suffering, they weren't self-absorbed. In his excellent book, *Disappointment with God*, Philip Yancey quotes William Barclay, who observed, "Endurance is not just the ability to bear a hard thing, but to turn it into glory." The believers were turning a hard thing into glory.

The leaders of the church still in Jerusalem heard great reports about people coming to Christ up the coast. They heard good news from Antioch and sent Barnabas to investigate. He may have realized that this was the perfect time and place for Paul to get involved, so he went to Tarsus. The two men spent a year in Antioch teaching and leading people to Christ.

During that time, another calamity affected the church, and it devastated the entire Roman world. A prophet named Agabus predicted that a famine would ravage the land, a famine that would occur just a few years later. In response, the believers didn't just sit around and complain. Luke tells us, "The disciples, each according to his ability, decided to provide help for the brothers living in Judea. This they did, sending their gift to the elders by Barnabas and Saul" (Acts 11:29-30). Where did the disciples learn to give like that? I'd guess that they picked up that kind of heart and generosity from Barnabas. Do you remember where we first met Barnabas in Luke's narrative? He sold his property and gave it to the church to provide for people's needs. Now he's multiplying his passion and heart in the lives of many others.

How could persecution and famine be strategic opportunities for the church? Because the believers trusted God, pitched in to help, and reaped a harvest of new believers. The Jewish historian Josephus and other writers record two plagues that devastated the Roman world in the first two centuries. As many as one-fourth to one-third of the people died in each one. In fear for their lives, the pagans who had hope only in this life, fled their homes and families, leaving the sick behind to fend for themselves. Of course, many of those left behind died from the combination of disease and neglect. In his book, The Rise of Christianity, Rodney Stark explains the reason why most of the Christians stayed to help the sick. They knew that if they died, they'd go to be with the Lord. Their faith in Christ helped them overcome their fears. Though many of the believers died from the disease, they were able to care for the unbelievers, many of whom recovered from their illness and came to Christ as a result of the love and care shown to them. When the first famine struck, Christians comprised only six to eight percent of the population. By the time the second famine was over, their numbers were as high as fifty percent. The increase was due to lives spared from disease and souls redeemed by grace. Their faith and love in dark times changed the world.

None of us would welcome persecution, famine, or disease, but God used all three to reach countless people with the good news of the gospel. These are times when spiritual opportunities are cleverly disguised as calamities. The key, though, was the ability of the Christians to look beyond the hardships and disappointments to "trust God no matter what." In hard times, nobody cares what color the carpet is in the church or what music style is used. They only care that we love them enough to step into their lives. A friend of mine lives on the Gulf Coast. He said that he lives in a typical neighborhood. He knows a few neighbors very well, but he has hardly even met some others. When a hurricane devastated his community, power was out for a week, roofs had been torn off, and trees were uprooted in almost every yard. He told me, "It was an amazing time. All of us were outside helping each other cut down trees, put tarps over holes in roofs, rebuild fences, and clean up all the debris that littered our neighborhood. Several of us went from one house to the next helping each other with chain saws and posthole diggers. I got to know my neighbors better in a week than I had in the previous fifteen years."

How do we make a difference in our neighborhoods? Yes, it's nice for churches to have attractive buildings, good music, and great teaching, but I believe what really matters is when we get outside ourselves to touch the lives of people in need. Every problem, every heartache, every setback is a God-given opportunity to show the love of Christ to someone.

When Agabus predicted the famine, the believers didn't wait until it happened to take action. They jumped in and took up a collection so the resources would be there when the needs arose. And they gave "each according to his ability," without guilt and as generously as possible.

On a few occasions, God prepared people for action by giving them a specific prophecy, but more often, the Christians never saw what was coming. For example, Peter and John had no idea they'd be arrested for healing a crippled man, and Paul didn't know (but he might have guessed) that he'd face such opposition after escaping over the city wall in a basket. We may not be able to anticipate an event, but we can always be prepared to respond in faith to any blessing or calamity. God doesn't protect Christians from famines, hurricanes, and economic downturns. We're not immune from the problems of life, but God gives us the grace to respond in faith.

The most strategic thing we can do is ask the Spirit of God to show us needs in people's lives, then step in with kindness, grace, and resources. When we do, we'll see God do amazing things in the lives of those we touch. When we get a taste of him using us, we won't even think about 50 hours and $50. We'll want to give him everything we are and everything we have, and we'll trust that he'll use both blessings and heartache to accomplish his purposes. That's normal. Successful ministry happens when heart preparation meets crying needs in people's lives. Are you there?

In hard times—individually or nationally—do we gripe, or do we trust God, make ourselves available, and meet the needs of those around us? If we're listening to the Spirit, God may prepare us for times of trouble, but even if he doesn't, we can respond with a warm heart, a word of hope, and an open wallet to meet the needs of others. It's normal for Christ-followers to be aware of the strategic opportunities God uses even in the midst of seemingly abnormal circumstances.

✞ Read Acts 11:19-30.

✞ How do you normally respond to difficulties? How does your response propel you to effective ministry or block it?

✞ When have you seen people draw closer in times of trouble? How did God use suffering and hardship to soften hearts and build relationships?

✞ Why is it crucial to have an eternal perspective in order to respond to difficulties with faith and hope?

✞ Compete the following prayer: "Lord Jesus, I complain much too often. Help me see difficulties in my life and in the lives of others as strategic opportunities to magnify your glory. Today, I trust you to…"

DAY SEVENTEEN | **NO GUARANTEES**

"It was about this time that King Herod arrested some who belonged to the church, intending to persecute them. He had James, the brother of John, put to death with the sword. When he saw that this pleased the Jews, he proceeded to seize Peter also. The night before Herod was to bring him to trial, Peter was sleeping between two soldiers, bound with two chains, and sentries stood guard at the entrance. Suddenly an angel of the Lord appeared and a light shone in the cell. He struck Peter on the side and woke him up. 'Quick, get up!' he said, and the chains fell off Peter's wrists" (Acts 12:1-3, 6-7).

Following Christ with our whole heart doesn't guarantee the outcomes we'd always like. That's a hard lesson for American Christians. Too many of us misunderstand God's will and his ways. We think that we have the right to prosperity if we trust God. The longer we walk with God and the more we read the Scriptures, we find that God's ways are sometimes mysterious—even baffling. At those times, we simply bow our heads and acknowledge that he's God, and we're not. When Jesus told his disciples that he was going to die for the sins of the world, Peter said, "No way!" but Jesus rebuked him, "Get behind me, Satan! You are a stumbling block to me; you do not have in mind the things of God, but the things of men" (Matthew 16:23).

During the persecution of the believers, King Herod sided with the Jewish authorities against The Way. As a political move to increase his power and popularity, he arrested James, the brother of John, and executed him with a sword. You may recall that before Jesus' crucifixion, the mother of James and John had come to Jesus to ask for a favor: "Grant that one of these two sons of mine may sit at your right hand and the other at your left in the kingdom" (Matthew 20:21).

Jesus must have shaken his head in dismay. They still thought he was leading a political movement, but he did not come to command that kind of power. He replied to her, "You don't know what you are asking." He then turned to the young men and asked, "Can you drink the cup I am going to drink?"

They answered, "Yes," so he told them plainly, "You will indeed drink from my cup, but to sit at my right or left is not for me to grant. These places belong to those for whom they have been prepared by my Father" (Matthew 20:23). Understandably, the other ten disciples were furious at the brothers and their mom. Jesus used the conflict to teach them (again) about the necessity of having a servant's heart.

Now in the early church, James drank of the cup Jesus had to drink at the cross. Many years later, John would drink it, too, when he died as an exile on the island of Patmos.

Of course, we prefer unlimited and unblemished health, wealth, and happiness, but God never promised those things. Jesus promised his presence and inner strength as we go through tribulations. As we walk with Christ, his grace increasingly shapes our desires, and we care more for his glory than our comfort. In fact, we realize difficulties are the path of spiritual growth, so we begin to welcome them as tutors to teach us life's most important lessons. We pray, but the focus of our prayers change from our happiness to a heartfelt desire that God receive honor and fame. Gradually, we come to the conclusion that life isn't about us any more—it's about Christ. Paul explained this point in his letter to the Christians in Rome: "For none of us lives to himself alone and none of us dies to himself alone. If we live, we live to the Lord; and if we die, we die to the Lord. So, whether we live or die, we belong to the Lord" (Romans 14:7-8). The most important fact of our life isn't the catalogue of our possessions, accomplishments, or awards. God may give us those things, but we hold them lightly. The thing we grip tightly is the magnificent truth that we belong to the King of kings!

After Herod killed James, he realized he had a winning public relations strategy. The Jews were thrilled that one of the Twelve had been executed, so Herod arrested Peter. Taking no chances, he assigned sixteen soldiers to guard Peter. (Maybe they didn't understand how harmless the fisherman was. When he tried to defend Jesus at the arrest, he missed his mark and cut off a man's ear. Peter wasn't much of a warrior!)

Believers in Jerusalem were well aware that James was dead, and now their beloved Peter was facing a similar end. The bleakness of the situation didn't discourage them; instead, they prayed with even more intensity. In the night, an angel appeared in the cell, and the light of the glory of God shined brightly. Peter must have been a heavy sleeper because the angel had to slap him on his side to wake him up! The angel told him, "Quick, get up!" and the chains fell from Peter's wrists.

The angel led Peter past the guards and out of the prison. When they came to the heavy iron gates, they opened without anyone touching them. When they had walked a block or two, the angel vanished, leaving Peter standing in the street alone. He assumed he had been seeing a vision similar to the one of the sheets just before he met Cornelius, but now he realized this was the real thing. He said to himself, "Now I know without a doubt that the Lord sent his angel and rescued me from Herod's clutches and from everything the Jewish people were anticipating" (Acts 12:11).

In one of the more comical moments in Luke's account, Peter found his way to the door of Mary, the mother of John Mark and the aunt of Barnabas, and probably the place where Jesus had held the Last Supper with his disciples. There was no angel to open the door, so he knocked. She recognized his voice, but in her shock and joy, she didn't open the door. She ran back to tell the others that their prayers had been answered. They responded, "You're out of your mind! It must be his angel."

Peter patiently kept knocking at the door. I can imagine him shifting his feet, whistling, and waiting for someone to come back to open the door for him. He must have knocked for a long time, but finally, they opened the door and let him in. What a story he had to tell!

What do we learn from the contrast between the outcomes for James and Peter? Did people pray for Peter but not for James? I doubt it. I'm sure they prayed that God would spare both men. Was the quality of their faith greater when they prayed for Peter than when they prayed for James? No, from Luke's description, they didn't believe God had freed Peter when the servant first told them. When they finally realized Peter had been released, do you think they believed their prayers were the cause of his freedom? Not at all, they had prayed just as fervently for James, but he was cruelly executed. What, then, could they conclude? That God's ways are far bigger and more mysterious than our finite minds can comprehend. The purpose of prayer isn't to twist God's arm and get him to jump through our hoops, but to transform our hearts, tap into his will, ask him to accomplish things that honor him, and celebrate his goodness.

There's nothing in the world wrong with asking God for blessings. We ask God to heal the sick, bring lost people to him, to bless our businesses, and to work in countless other ways. But it's not our prayers that change things; it's God. Our prayers aren't powerful; God is. We never demand that God do this or that. We simply pour out our hearts to him, ask him to do what only he can do, and we humbly accept his will. At one point in Paul's life, he suffered physical pain from a "thorn in the flesh." He asked God to take it away, but God said, "No." The lesson Paul learned, though, was much richer and deeper than a simple "No." God explained, "My grace is sufficient for you, for my power is made perfect in weakness." Paul concluded, "Therefore I will boast all the more gladly about my weaknesses, so that Christ's power may rest on me. That is why, for Christ's sake, I delight in weaknesses, in insults, in hardships, in persecutions, in difficulties. For when I am weak, then I am strong" (2 Corinthians 12:9-10).

For centuries, believers have been taught to end our prayers with the phrase, "in Jesus' name, amen." Sometimes, we just say these words without thinking, but a little reflection brings a lot of light. The term "in Jesus' name" carries three important aspects of meaning. It means we're praying as God's child, in his will, and for his honor.

When we pray, we can remember that we're God's beloved children. He has proved his love for us, and he has given us intimacy and access to him. We come before the throne of God with our requests like a child goes to her father to ask for things.

Our requests, however, must always be guided by the will of God. As we pray, we ask God for wisdom about what he wants. Quite often, our times of prayer show us that our hearts need a little (or maybe a lot) of work. Like Jesus in the garden, we have to be willing to say, "Not my will, Lord, but yours." When Paul prayed for the Colossians, he asked God to fill them "with the knowledge of his will through all spiritual wisdom and understanding" (Colossians 1:9). That's not a bad prayer for us, too!

And as we pray, God sometimes shows us that our sense of purpose needs some work. We may want God to answer our prayers to make our lives more comfortable, or maybe so that we can show people what great Christians we are. When the Holy Spirit shines his light on your impure motives, don't be alarmed. It happens to all of us. Take the correction to heart, and make a commitment to honor God with your prayer and your words.

So, what's normal in our prayers? We realize that there are no guarantees. When we ask God for anything, we should realize that he may well say "No" or "Wait." God's ways are sometimes crystal clear, but sometimes they are mysterious. We may feel led to give sacrificially just before we lose our job. We may long for a good medical report, but receive bad news. But we keep on praying as his child, in his will, and for his glory.

And sometimes, God answers our prayers in a way that causes us to shake our heads in amazement and praise his name. A young woman who grew up in a solid family and a good church lost her way in college. She began drinking and smoking pot, and loved to party with her new friends. When she graduated, she moved to another city, and got hooked up with a drug dealer. They lived together, and, as a result, she began using harder drugs. Her parents and their friends prayed fervently for her. They begged her to change and reminded her of God's love and the consequences of her sins. Nothing they said made a dent. She became furious with them. After three years living with the pusher, she became pregnant. Several months later as her delivery approached, she came home to her parents and broke down in tears. She wept, "I can't bring up my child in a hellhole like that."

Over the next year, God did an amazing work in her life. She kept the baby, got a job, and began trusting God. She attended Bible studies and support groups. Her father remarked one day, "I haven't seen this light in her eyes since she was in high school." About two years later, her high school sweetheart called her. They hadn't seen each other in seven years, but he had heard what had happened to her. He came to see her, and they began dating. A few months later, he shocked her by asking her to marry him. She asked, "Why do you want to marry somebody like me?"

He looked into her eyes and replied, "I've been waiting for you all these years. I don't care what you've done or where you've been. I love you."

This young woman, her son, and her new husband have joined a great church and are living testimonies of the grace of God. Her parents and their friends are like the people in the house where Peter was knocking on the door after God sent an angel to release him—they prayed long and hard, and when God answered, they could hardly believe God worked so miraculously!

Sadly, there are plenty of other parents who prayed just as fervently for their prodigal child, and the son or daughter never returned. When we pray, it's entirely normal to be confused from time to time. Quite often, God uses our times of prayer to change us more than he changes the situation, but sometimes he changes both.

⊹ **Read Acts 12:1-19.**

⊹ **When have you prayed fervently and been disappointed? How did the experience shape your faith (positively or negatively)?**

⊹ **What does it mean to pray "in Jesus' name"?**

⊹ **What are some things (maybe only one) that you are desperate for God to do right now in your life, or in the life of someone you love? How will the lessons of today help you pray?**

⊹ **Complete the following prayer: "Lord Jesus, I want to learn to pray more expectantly, but also, with fewer demands that you do what I want you to do. Today, I want to..."**

DAY EIGHTEEN
RELENTLESS LOVE

"When the Gentiles heard this, they were glad and honored the word of the Lord; and all who were appointed for eternal life believed. The word of the Lord spread through the whole region. But the Jews incited the God-fearing women of high standing and the leading men of the city. They stirred up persecution against Paul and Barnabas, and expelled them from their region. So they shook the dust from their feet in protest against them and went to Iconium. And the disciples were filled with joy and with the Holy Spirit" (Acts 13:48-52).

Whatever it takes, that was the attitude of Jesus, and it was Paul's perspective as well. Jesus was willing to humble himself, take off the robes of heaven, and put on swaddling cloths in a manger to connect with us. As he walked the earth, he met with all kinds of people: the rich and the poor, the sick and the well, the insiders and the outsiders. He wanted to share his love with every person on the planet, but his strategy was to start with God's chosen people, the Jews. They had the background in truth and experience with God. They could be the spring-board of world evangelization—if they were willing.

Paul had been the most reluctant convert to Christ. (By the way, Luke now calls him Paul, his Roman name, instead of Saul, his Jewish name.) He conspired against Christians until that fateful day when Jesus appeared to him on the road to Damascus. After a time of preparation, he was ready to take the message of God's grace to the Gentiles. His strategy was like Jesus'. In each city, he first went to the synagogues to help the Jews understand that Jesus was the fulfillment of all the laws and promises they had believed for centuries. If they became believers, they would have a head start on faith, theology, and holiness.

Paul and Barnabas had been teaching and ministering in Antioch, but the Lord had bigger plans for them. As the believers prayed, the Holy Spirit gave orders to "set apart" these two men for a special mission. The Spirit directed them to Cyprus and then to the south coast of present day Turkey. When they left the ship, they traveled by land to the city of Pisidian Antioch. On the Sabbath, they went to the synagogue. Following the regular reading of the law and the prophets, one of the rulers of the synagogue told them, "Brothers, if you have a message of encouragement for the people, please speak" (Acts 13:15).

Never at a loss for words, Paul launched into a detailed account of God's plan to redeem Israel, and through Israel, the whole world. He explained that Jesus was the fulfillment of all the promises and prophecy. At the end, he told them, "Therefore, my brothers, I want you to know that through Jesus the forgiveness of sins is proclaimed to you. Through him everyone who believes is justified from everything you could not be justified from by the law of Moses" (Acts 13:38-39).

Many who heard Paul that day wanted to hear more, and by the next Sabbath, "almost the whole city" turned out to hear him preach and teach about Jesus. The Jewish leaders were jealous, and they condemned Paul and Barnabas. Plan A had failed. Paul had hoped that the Jews in the city would believe and become the light of Christ to those around them, but they rejected Jesus as their Messiah, even though he had reminded the Jews that they were missing out on God's grand design for them. He quoted Isaiah, "I have made you a light to the Gentiles, that you may bring salvation to the ends of the earth" (Isaiah 49:6 and Acts 13:47). Paul and Barnabas now turned to Plan B, which was to go directly to the Gentiles in the area.

The Gentiles were thrilled to hear that God loved them and offered forgiveness, purpose, and eternal life. Many people believed, and in response, the Jews were even more furious. They conspired against Paul and Barnabas and ran them out of town. The faith of the new believers, though, was strong. Luke tells us, "And the disciples were filled with joy and with the Holy Spirit" (Acts 13:52).

I love to see people have a "whatever it takes" attitude. Before Christmas, my friends, Wayne and Kristy Northup, decided to step out and do something risky for God. We had our usual big outreach to help disadvantaged people in our area, and they knew that the people in our church would meet every need. They prayed and asked God for direction. Soon God impressed upon them to find a family in Dallas who needed help for the holidays. The problem was that they didn't know who that family might be. They Googled "Family who needs help during Christmas in Dallas," and they found a website that connected families in need with those who would like to help.

An ad on the website read: "Bethany—a twenty-six year-old single mother with two kids: a five year-old son and a four year-old daughter. Needs groceries."

Wayne connected with the young mom and asked if he and Kristy could cook a big Christmas dinner for her and her children. Instead of inviting Bethany and her family to their home, he asked if he, Kristy, and their children could take everything they had prepared to her apartment and eat with them.

Bethany gladly agreed to let them into her home. Libby, their daughter, wrapped some of her favorite toys to give to Bethany's little girl. Kristy bought some gift cards and gifts for Bethany and her son, and they headed to her home for Christmas dinner.

Before they sat down for dinner, the two families took some time to get to know each other. Bethany said she had been working as a dental hygienist, but had recently lost her job and was trying to make ends meet. When Kristy asked her about her spiritual background, she smiled and shrugged, "I guess I really don't have one."

Wayne asked if she and her children would like him to read the Christmas story. She said, "Sure, but I don't have a Bible. To be honest, I've only been to church once in my life." Wayne had brought his Bible, and the two families listened intently as he read the story of Jesus' birth. When he was finished, he asked if he could pray before they sat down to eat. They had a wonderful meal together, and Bethany's kids thoroughly enjoyed opening the presents.

A couple of months later, Bethany and her children showed up one Sunday morning at our Mesquite church campus. It was surely a "coincidence" that Wayne was speaking that day. At the end of the service, he gave an invitation for people to put their trust in Christ. Bethany came forward and made a decision to give her heart to the Lord.

God has been at work in this little family. It all happened because a couple, touched by the love of God, wanted to share that love with people who needed to experience the kindness and grace of God. Wayne and Kristy wanted to have an incarnational ministry representing the reality of Christ's presence wherever they went. They could have just given money to the church, or have cooked a nice meal for a family—but they wanted to embrace people who were, by any measure, outcasts and unknowns in our culture.

It has always been God's design for his people to bless the whole world. That was his promise to Abraham, to David, through the prophets, and to the nation of Israel. Now it's his plan for the church. Some of us have a minimalist approach. We want to do just enough so that we don't feel guilty before God or ashamed if anyone asks what we've done. I believe God wants far more than for us to check off some boxes on our spiritual list of requirements. The adventure of walking with God in a rich and vibrant relationship, means giving everything we've got to the Lord and trusting him to direct us to people in need.

We can hold back from reaching out to others. We can protect ourselves from disappointment and avoid inconvenience, but when we avoid those risks, we also block the flow of God's Spirit to lead us. If we're open to God and responsive to the Spirit's prompting, he'll lead us to people we previously didn't know exist, or maybe to a next door neighbor, or perhaps a child or spouse or parent who needs to experience the touch of Jesus from us.

Paul and Barnabas had a Plan A to enlist other Jews to take the love of God to everyone around them, but when the Jews refused to budge, they were ready to put Plan B into effect. And you know, Plan B is pretty good. You and I are products of that plan, and God is still using anyone willing to put themselves in his hands.

✧ **Read Acts 13:1-52.**

✧ **What does it mean to have a positive, optimistic, "whatever it takes" attitude as we respond to God?**

✧ **Is your love for people relentless? Why or why not?**

✧ **Who is a good example for you of this kind of optimism and radical love for others? What does that person do to demonstrate love to others?**

✧ **Complete the following prayer: "Jesus, fill me with your relentless love so that it overflows from me. Today, I want to…"**

DAY NINETEEN | FICKLE PRAISE

> "When the crowd saw what Paul had done, they shouted in the Lycaonian language, 'The gods have come down to us in human form!' . . . Then some Jews came from Antioch and Iconium and won the crowd over. They stoned Paul and dragged him outside the city, thinking he was dead" (Acts 14:11, 19).

It's amazing how quickly people's perceptions can change. When Jesus entered Jerusalem on Palm Sunday, he rode on a colt's back to the cheers of the people, but only a few days later, the crowd was yelling, "Crucify him!" Luke describes a series of events in Acts that rivals this pivot in people's perspectives.

Paul and Barnabas had been kicked out of Pisidian Antioch so they went to Iconium where a crowd of people believed in Christ. Again, the Jewish leaders became jealous and plotted to kill them. They fled the city and shared the good news about Jesus in nearby cities. When they arrived in Lystra, they saw a man who had been crippled from birth. He listened carefully to Paul, and Paul discerned that the man had faith to be made well. He said, "Stand up on your feet!" The man jumped up and walked (Acts 14:10).

The crowd was amazed. They'd never seen anything like this, and they assumed Paul and Barnabas were gods. Luke paints the picture for us: "Barnabas they called Zeus, and Paul they called Hermes because he was the chief speaker. The priest of Zeus, whose temple was just outside the city, brought bulls and wreaths to the city gates because he and the crowd wanted to offer sacrifices to them" (Acts 14:12-13).

Talk about making a good first impression! But the missionary partners would have nothing of it. "But when the apostles Barnabas and Paul heard of this, they tore their clothes and rushed out into the crowd, shouting: 'Men, why are you doing this? We too are only men, human like you' " (Acts 14:14-15). They saw this moment as an opportunity to tell the adoring throng about Jesus, but even when they told them clearly that it was Jesus who had healed the lame man, the people still wanted to sacrifice bulls to them.

The next sentence in Luke's history tells us that it didn't take much to change the crowd's minds. "Then some Jews came from Antioch and Iconium and won the crowd over. They stoned Paul and dragged him outside the city, thinking he was dead" (Acts 14:19). The disciples stood around him, probably wondering where they were going to bury him, but suddenly, Paul got up, but didn't run away. He went back into the city and preached Christ again before leaving the next day with Barnabas.

One of the chief sources of our identity is the acclaim of others, but we need to realize that it's as fickle and fleeting as the crowd at Lystra. Many of us carefully craft our lives to please others. We wear just the right clothes, go to the right places, say the right things, drive the right car, and hang out with the right people—all with the compelling desire to win approval from certain individuals we admire or fear. How can we tell if we're living for approval? When we don't get it, or we fear losing it, we respond in panic. Our thoughts are absorbed with pleasing others to win their respect, we work hard to win accolades and prove we're worth their applause, or we hide to keep people from knowing how flawed we really are. We wear masks all day every day to make sure people are impressed with us, but soon we don't even know who we are. We actually become the mask: superficial and hollow.

It's important for us to have a right view of ourselves so that we avoid both self-righteousness and self-pity—both of which are types of destructive pride. Humility isn't beating ourselves up, but accepting God's evaluation of ourselves. The Scriptures say we are wonderfully created, deeply loved, tragically fallen and flawed, gloriously redeemed, and warmly accepted by God. We aren't what we should be, but by the grace of God we aren't what we used to be, and as we look to eternity, we're not yet what we will be.

True humility enables us to accept compliments without making a big deal of them. We can simply say, "Thank you. I appreciate it." False humility causes us to discount the nice things people say about us. Instead of accepting them, we say something like, "Oh, it wasn't really that good," or "It wasn't me; it was the Lord." It's not pride to acknowledge that God has used us. He saved us, gifted us, equipped us, and we made ourselves available. Everything we do is for him, through him, and in him. And every talent is God's design in us. Leon Dillinger is a missionary who parachuted into the interior of Irian Jaya many years ago. He not only led many of the Dani tribe—including headhunters—to Christ, but he established a seminary and sent scores of students to nearby tribes to tell them about Jesus. When he tells his story of God's blessings, there's not a shred of pride or false humility. Someone asked him about the nature of humility, and he shared a passage from one of Paul's letters to the Corinthians: "For who makes you different from anyone else? What do you have that you did not receive? And if you did receive it, why do you boast as though you did not?" (1 Corinthians 4:7) He explained that he never feels that he has to build himself up or tear himself down because God has given him every ability he possesses. That's a wonderful perspective on humility!

And when we receive criticism, we don't have to react defensively. We can take it in, think and pray about it, talk to a spouse or a close friend, and then determine if and how much of the criticism is valid. Strength of character helps us rise above petty arguments and paybacks to get even with those who said something (anything!) negative about us. When our identity is rooted in the love, forgiveness, and acceptance of God, we won't feel terribly threatened when people attack us, ignore us, or criticize us, and we'll realize that the compliments of people are really praises to God because he's the source of our abilities and opportunities.

If Paul and Barnabas had reacted to the praise of the people of Lystra like some of us, they would have said, "Bring it on! Kill those bulls, and build us a temple. This is what I've always wanted, and I deserve it!" But longing for the praise of people makes us terribly vulnerable to two problems: rejection and comparison. We can easily identify attacks as outright rejection, but feeling ignored is almost worse. When people attack us, at least they acknowledge that we exist! Those who feel abandoned often have trouble knowing how deep the wound really is. But a more common problem in our lives today is comparison. We compare everything about our lives, from our teeth and cars to our diplomas and golf swings. Nothing is off limits! Even when we think we're winning this game, we're losing because our focus is in the wrong place. We need to get off this treadmill, realize the destructiveness of our heart's deception, and put our focus where it belongs—on the grace of God.

As we think about this passage, we also need to remember to avoid painting people as black or white, perfect or villainous, putting people too high on a pedestal or talking about them like they're Nazi murderers. To be sure, there are a few genuinely evil people, but most of the people we meet each day at home, at school, at work, and in our neighborhoods, are a shade of gray. If we see them clearly, we'll appreciate the fact that they, too, are wonderfully created, deeply loved, tragically fallen and flawed, gloriously redeemed, and warmly accepted by God.

The more we step up to honor God with our lives, the more we'll expose ourselves to the fickle opinions of others. Some will praise us when we succeed, and some (maybe the same ones) will condemn us when we fail—or if they perceive we've failed. The higher we climb in leadership, the more distorted we can expect people's views of us to be. We don't have to have titles to be leaders. If we're giving 50 hours and $50 to the cause of Christ, we're taking bold initiative to make a difference, and people are watching. Enjoy every minute of it. When you see God working in and through you, tell the world about it and give glory to God. Whenever the Holy Spirit shows you that you linger a bit too long over people's praise or you agonize too much over their criticism, think about the importance of true humility that comes from an accurate self-appraisal, one that is based on God's grace and gifts, not your ability or inability to impress people. Live for the audience of One.

When I was a boy, my father took me aside one day to talk to me. It was one of those conversations I knew I'd always remember. He said, "Son, God's hand is on you, and I believe he wants to use you to accomplish some great things. I have three important lessons I want you to remember for the rest of your life. Are you ready for them?"

I swallowed hard and said, "Yes, Dad. I'm ready."

He looked me in the eye and said, "Stay humble, stay holy, and keep your horse in the barn." I must have looked at him like I was confused because he laughed and explained, "I'm not worried about that last one, but I sure want you to focus on the other two. Son, pride is deceptive. If you aren't careful, you'll fall into the trap of thinking that your success has come from your gifts and your wisdom, and you'll think you deserve praise for it. Remember: 'For thine is the kingdom, and the power, and the glory.' "

I love the story of Henri Nouwen, the Notre Dame professor, who left the prestige of his position at the height of his acclaim to care for Adam, a man with special needs. Nouwen explains his relationship with Adam this way:

"Adam is a twenty-five year old man who cannot speak, cannot dress or undress himself, cannot walk alone, cannot eat without much help. He does not cry or laugh. Only occasionally does he make eye contact. His back is distorted. His arm and leg movements are twisted. He suffers from severe epilepsy and, despite heavy medication, sees few days without grand-mal seizures. Sometimes, as he grows suddenly rigid, he utters a howling groan. On a few occasions, I've seen one big tear roll down his cheek.

It takes me about an hour and a half to wake Adam up, give him his medication, carry him into his bath, wash him, shave him, clean his teeth, dress him, walk him to the kitchen, give him his breakfast, put him in his wheelchair and bring him to the place where he spends most of the day with therapeutic exercises."

Adam didn't care that Nouwen had been one of the most gifted and re-nowned teachers in the church. He only cared that Nouwen loved him enough to feed him, clothe him, talk to him, and care for his every need. When asked why he would give up his "more important" task of teaching in order to care for Adam, Nouwen responded, "I am not giving up anything… It is I, not Adam, who gets the main benefit from our relationship." Humility is caring for people and doing the right thing when no one even notices, because we're convinced that there's always One who notices, and only his opinion counts.

✚ Read Acts 14:1-20.

✚ How would you define and describe arrogance and false humility?

✚ How does comparison wreck a person's sense of stability, identity, and relationships? What are some things that you're tempted to compare with others?

✚ How would it change your thought life and your identity if you were convinced that you are wonderfully created, deeply loved, tragically fallen and flawed, gloriously redeemed, and warmly accepted by God?

✚ Complete the following prayer: "Jesus, I want to live wholeheartedly for you, not for the praise of people or in fear of their criticism. Today, help me to…"

DAY TWENTY | **THE RISK OF GRACE**

> "Then some of the believers who belonged to the party of the Pharisees stood up and said, 'The Gentiles must be circumcised and required to obey the law of Moses.' The apostles and elders met to consider this question" (Acts 15:5-6).

It happened in the first decades of the church's life, it's happened in every generation since then, and it's happening again today. Wherever the amazing grace of God has been preached, there are always some people who feel uncomfortable with it and want to make the Christian faith little more than a bunch of rules to follow. They feel completely justified by their demands. Doesn't the Bible give commands to be holy, with lists of do's and don'ts? Grace has always been a risky proposition for God. People have the option to walk away, to misunderstand, and to take advantage of him by claiming his forgiveness gives them freedom to sin all they want. In reaction to these flagrant abuses of God's kindness and leniency, some church leaders throughout the ages have said, "No more! We're going to make sure nobody who claims to be a Christian will go off track!" But God seems to be perfectly willing to take the risk of extending grace again and again.

The big question in the early church was whether Gentiles could be Christians, and if they were, how should they relate to the Jewish customs that were the foundation of the nation of Israel and, some thought, the new sect of The Way? In one of the cities which Paul and Barnabas had preached Christ and led many Gentiles to faith, came Jewish believers who put a heavy load on the new believers: "Unless you are circumcised according to the custom taught by Moses, you cannot be saved" (Acts 15:1). There it was, with no subtlety in the debate. The battle lines were clearly drawn, and Paul and Barnabas were ready. They weren't going to let some narrow, legalistic, self-righteous teachers destroy all they had done to bring the message of God's grace to the Gentiles.

The debate became so intense that it threatened the whole enterprise. World evangelism hung on the answer. The church leaders sent Paul and Barnabas to Jerusalem for the first great council of the faith. The discussion became heated, and then Peter spoke up. He told the counsel, "Brothers, you know that some time ago God made a choice among you that the Gentiles might hear from my lips the message of the gospel and believe. God, who knows the heart, showed that he accepted them by giving the Holy Spirit to them, just as he did to us. He made no distinction between us and them, for he purified their hearts by faith. Now then, why do you try to test God by putting on the necks of the disciples a yoke that neither we nor our fathers have been able to bear? No! We believe it is through the grace of our Lord Jesus that we are saved, just as they are" (Acts 15:7-11).

When Peter sat down, Paul and Barnabas told story after story of Gentiles coming to Christ and how the Spirit was poured out on them—without them being circumcised, following Jewish customs, or obeying Jewish laws of diet and worship. James summed up the counsel's answer in a letter affirming the supremacy of God's grace. To build bridges between the Jewish and Gentile camps, he instructed the Gentiles to avoid the sins most abhorrent to the Jews. The letter was sent to Antioch where the debate began, and the Gentile believers were thrilled (and I'm sure, relieved).

Why do we gravitate to rules instead of grace? One reason is because rule keeping is easier to quantify and measure, especially when compared to objective goals. When we meet the standards, we can feel good about ourselves, and when we fail, the remedy seems clear. The problem is that God wants far more than people who try to prove their value by keeping a set of rules. He wants our hearts. When Jesus was asked, "What is the greatest commandment in the law?" he responded, "Love the Lord your God with all your heart, soul and mind." He didn't give a catalog of all six hundred or so laws in the Old Testament, and he didn't say, "Yeah, and I've got a bunch more for you now." The fiercest arguments we find in the gospels were between Jesus, who kept pointing people to grace and love, and the religious leaders, who insisted on rules being the way we earn points with God. The message of grace is that we can never, ever keep all the rules. It's hopeless, and we're helpless. The rules, Paul told the Galatians, are our tutors to teach us the important lesson that we're sinners in desperate need of a Savior. Rules are not the source of salvation, but the awareness of sin.

The Christians in Galatia had forgotten the supremacy of grace. To Paul, their slip into legalism wasn't a minor matter. He scolded them, "I am astonished that you are so quickly deserting the one who called you by the grace of Christ and are turning to a different gospel—which is really no gospel at all. Evidently some people are throwing you into confusion and are trying to pervert the gospel of Christ. But even if we or an angel from heaven should preach a gospel other than the one we preached to you, let him be eternally condemned! As we have already said, so now I say again: If anybody is preaching to you a gospel other than what you accepted, let him be eternally condemned!" (Galatians 1:6-9) Later in his letter, he told them clearly, "I do not set aside the grace of God, for if righteousness could be gained through the law, Christ died for nothing" (Galatians 2:21).

Jesus and Paul never said that the law, the rules for living, and the guidelines throughout the Bible aren't important. They are, but they aren't of supreme importance or the source of change. They show us our sinfulness when we fail to meet them, so we turn to God's mercy and grace for forgiveness. Rules also show us how God wants us to live, so we trust him to give us strength and courage to obey. Genuine spiritual life comes from inside, from a transformation of our hearts by grace, not by strictly keeping a set of rules to show God and everybody else that we deserve honor. In a beautiful description of the way God changes hearts and then changes our behavior, Jesus spoke up at a major feast in Jerusalem. Each day, the ceremonies became more important, reaching a crescendo on the last day. John's gospel tells us, "On the last and greatest day of the Feast, Jesus stood and said in a loud voice, 'If anyone is thirsty, let him come to me and drink. Whoever believes in me, as the Scripture has said, streams of living water will flow from within him.' By this he meant the Spirit, whom those who believed in him were later to receive" (John 7:37-39).

If we're thirsty for God's presence, pardon, and power in our lives, we don't look to rules to quench our thirst. We drink in Christ himself. We respond to his love by loving him back. We marvel at his willingness to sacrifice for us, and we adore him even more. With a full heart of gratitude, we want to please him in every way we can. That's where the rules fit in—not as a means of salvation, but to give us direction as we gladly express the salvation we've experienced.

How can we tell if we're living by grace or by rules? People who try to earn points by keeping rules feel superior to anyone they perceive isn't keeping the right ones or keeping them as well as they are. Rule-keepers are judgmental, critical, and arrogant. When they fail, they beat themselves up and promise God they'll do better. They don't experience the cleansing and refreshment of God's forgiveness; they just recommit themselves to try harder next time. Before long, these people develop deep resentments and bitterness. They are angry at those who seem to really enjoy their relationship with God. In stark contrast, theirs is a grind.

On the other hand, those who take God at his word and understand that he offers free, unbridled love and forgiveness bask in his grace, and long to please the one who loves them so much. They certainly aren't perfect, but when the Spirit shows them a sinful attitude or behavior, they aren't defensive. They admit their sin, feel appropriate sorrow for grieving God's heart, and accept his unlimited forgiveness. Confession and repentance doesn't shatter their faith. It reinforces and deepens their grasp of God's grace, and it causes them to love him and want to obey him even more.

When grace is taught and modeled, amazing things can happen. Not long ago, some kids in a youth group became judgmental of some other students who had recently come to Christ but were still drinking and smoking pot. Some of the ones who had been believers longer told them, "If you're going to do that stuff, don't come to our youth group."

When I heard about it, I met with them and explained, "The people you're telling not to come are brand new believers. They don't understand yet what it means to walk with God. Give them a break. Show them the grace Christ has for them. As they grow, they'll learn what it means to follow him in every area of their lives. Now, if Keith, your leader, does that kind of thing, that's different. We'll kick his butt because God has a higher set of expectations for leaders than for new believers. But don't put roadblocks in the life of new Christians. Point them to Jesus, model a life of grace and holiness that comes from gratitude, and watch God work in their lives."

Mark Brewer was a bartender at Chili's. Richie Brown met him and brought him to hang out with some of us. Before long, Mark accepted Richie's invitation to come to church, and he gave his heart to the Lord. He realized his current lifestyle wasn't helping him follow Christ, so he moved out of his apartment and moved into the vacant evangelist's quarters at our church. After a few weeks, a lady came up to me with a strange expression on her face. She said, "Pastor Scott, uh, I think you might need to talk to Mark."

"About what?" I asked.

"About his other job."

"I don't know what you mean." I was still completely clueless.

She finally had the courage to explain, "I saw him in the mall modeling bikini underwear for a store there."

I instantly reacted, "No way!"

She nodded, "Yes, I'm sure it was him."

The next day, I found Mark and asked him about it. He immediately said, "Yeah, it's pretty good money. What's the problem?"

I told him, "Brother, you can't do that. It's not right to expose yourself. I know you have the whole 'six pack' thing going, but don't do that any more."

Without a shred of defensiveness, he answered, "No problem. I didn't know it was wrong. I won't do it again."

There were some other rough edges that needed to be filed off Mark's life, but he was willing to change because he was enamored with the grace of God. He wanted to please God with all his heart, so he was always open to changing his life as needed. That's the right way to look at grace as the motivation for obedience.

It's not that rules aren't important in the kingdom. They're important, but they're not central. The marvelous grace of God is the supreme truth about God and about our relationship with him. Many of us gravitate to rules to try to prove ourselves to people and earn points with God, but we have to fight this misunderstanding of the life of faith. Paul and Barnabas took the message to believers everywhere, to both Jews and Gentiles, that God is willing to take the risk of grace to win our hearts and enflame a genuine passion to please him because we love him so much. It was normal then, and it's normal now.

✚ Read Acts 15:1-41.

✚ How have you seen the negative characteristics of rule-keeping in people's lives, maybe your own?

✚ How is grace a more powerful motivation to obey God than rules could ever be? Why, then, do many of us gravitate toward rules?

✚ How are you doing in the fight to live by grace and not by rules?

✚ Complete the following prayer: "Jesus, you are beautiful to me. Your grace is amazing, and I want to let it overflow from me to everyone around me. Today, I need you to work it deep into my heart so that..."

DAY TWENTY-ONE
SUBMISSION

> "Paul and his companions traveled throughout the region of Phrygia and Galatia, having been kept by the Holy Spirit from preaching the word in the province of Asia. When they came to the border of Mysia, they tried to enter Bithynia, but the Spirit of Jesus would not allow them to. So they passed by Mysia and went down to Troas. During the night Paul had a vision of a man of Macedonia standing and begging him, 'Come over to Macedonia and help us'" (Acts 16:6-9).

As we read the Bible, we uncover the marvelous benefits of knowing and loving God. Some of the psalms tell how God has orchestrated the world to provide food, shelter, and clothing for us. The gospel of grace explains that God has forgiven us and adopted us into his family. These and many other blessings thrill our hearts. Sooner or later, though, we realize that following Christ demands that we put him first above all others. He won't settle for second place. We call him "Lord," which means master. Children who grasp the greatness of a powerful and loving father know they have lots of freedom to enjoy him and his gifts, but when there is any conflict of purposes, they have to submit to his will.

At one point in the life of Christ, three men came up to him. The first one volunteered to go with Jesus, but Jesus told him about the cost: "Foxes have holes and birds of the air have nests, but the Son of Man has no place to lay his head."

Jesus invited the other two men to follow him, but they both mumbled excuses. One wanted to wait until his father had died. His father, we realize, was more important than Jesus. The other similarly was too attached to people back home, and he wanted to put them first. Jesus told him plainly, "No one who puts his hand to the plow and looks back is fit for service in the kingdom of God" (Luke 9:57-62).

Following Christ is the most glorious and yet the most challenging thing we'll ever do. Again and again, God gives us a choice: our will or his, fulfilling our desires or pleasing him, being devoted to our comfort or his glory. If we're willing to say "Yes" to Christ in those choices, we necessarily say "No" to other things, often some good and pleasant things that fight for supremacy in our hearts. As we pick up the story in Acts, we see two important moments when people were asked to submit their wills to God.

The first tension point was about a promising young leader named Timothy. His mother was Jewish, and his father was Greek. For him to travel with Paul and minister to both Jews and Gentiles, Paul knew that the young man would have to break down every barrier between him and the people he wanted to reach. Since his father was Greek, Timothy had never been circumcised. Paul asked if he would be willing to undergo this surgery, and Timothy agreed. This was not an act to make him acceptable to God. Paul and Barnabas had defended grace in the Jerusalem council. This was about earning the right to be heard by a large audience of people—nothing more, but nothing less. When Paul asked Timothy to be circumcised, the young man had a choice: to submit to Paul's leadership and open a door to greater ministry, or choose comfort and convenience at the expense of ministry opportunities. He chose to submit, and God used him to open doors to the gospel in town after town as he traveled with Paul. Later, he became the pastor of the church at Ephesus and the recipient of two wonderful letters from Paul in the New Testament.

It's fascinating that we read the story of Timothy's submission to Paul's leadership and being circumcised immediately after the biggest debate in the early church settled the issue that Gentiles don't have to be circumcised. The point here isn't that Paul changed his mind, or that he doubted grace. Paul was the preeminent theologian of his day, and he wasn't backing down on grace a single inch. But in his mission to take the gospel to the whole world, he knew his fellow missionaries had to be culturally relevant. Timothy's circumcision was for that purpose alone. Young believers like Timothy need to pay attention to more mature leaders. It's the way young people gain wisdom and maturity. Peter wrote about this crucial connection: "Young men, in the same way be submissive to those who are older. All of you, clothe yourselves with humility toward one another, because, 'God opposes the proud but gives grace to the humble.' Humble yourselves, therefore, under God's mighty hand, that he may lift you up in due time" (1 Peter 5:5-6).

Submission is a normal part of the Christian life. We value individual freedoms in our country (especially in Texas), but all of us have to be willing to submit our wills to God, to our leadership, and to the government. Paul told the Christians in Rome, "Everyone must submit himself to the governing authorities, for there is no authority except that which God has established" (Romans 13:1). Even Jesus, the Lord of all, was submissive to Roman rule. When tax collectors asked if Jesus was going to pay the temple tax, Jesus explained that they didn't have to pay it, but they'd pay it to avoid offending people. He told Peter, "Then the sons are exempt. But so that we may not offend them, go to the lake and throw out your line. Take the first fish you catch; open its mouth and you will find a four-drachma coin. Take it and give it to them for my tax and yours" (Matthew 17:26-27). Peter and Jesus could have made their point and refused to pay, but Jesus knew there was a higher calling than winning an argument over taxes—winning the hearts of lost men and women.

The second example of submission is Paul's willingness to obey the whisper of the Spirit about his direction for ministry Paul was a go-getter. He wanted to take the word of Christ to places no one had ever been before. He wanted to preach in the province of Asia, today the central part of Turkey, but the Holy Spirit "prevented him" from going. He and his companions then tried to go to Bithynia, "but the Spirit of Jesus would not allow them to" (Acts 16:7). I can imagine Paul wondering, "What's going on? Jesus told me to take the gospel to the whole world, and now he won't let me go!" But we have no record of Paul's frustration. Maybe the grace of God and the previous experiences of being led by God gave him a large measure of patience. But God's "No" wasn't the end of the road by a long shot. In the night, God gave Paul a vision. A man from a region north of Greece, begged him, "Come over to Macedonia and help us" (Acts 16:9).

Luke, who joined Paul's party at this point, tells us that Paul, Silas, and the group sailed to Philippi, a Roman colony on the coast of Greece, where they led their first convert there to the Lord. The gospel had now made it to the continent of Europe.

We can always find plenty of good reasons to avoid submitting our wills to God, to godly authority, to each other, and to the government. The first sin recorded in the Bible was Eve's insistence on personal autonomy, to "be like God," and not be dependent on anything or submissive to anybody. Things haven't changed much. Deep in the heart of every human being is the same desire to be independent, to owe nothing to anyone, and to avoid submitting our wills at all costs.

I believe there's a difference, though, between submission and agreement. I've talked to people who said they have no problem with submission, but as we talked, I realized they agreed with their leader's decision. Submission is required when we disagree with the Lord or a leader, when obedience is costly, and when we're forced to examine our hearts to see if we're insisting on our wills instead of God's. The Hall of Faith in Hebrews 11 contains men and women who had to face their deepest fears and the shattering of their highest hopes, but they chose God's will over their own prestige, comfort, and the acclaim of others. That's submission.

There are, though, two different kinds of submission. One is obedience with a clenched fist and a defiant heart. A teacher had to tell a little boy in grade school to sit down over and over. Finally, she threatened him with the most severe punishment the school could deliver. A few minutes later, she saw him sitting in his seat, but his arms were folded and his eyes glared at her. She said, "Timmy, I appreciate your willingness to be obedient and sit down."

He snapped back, "I'm sitting down on the outside, but I'm standing up on the inside!"

When I struggle with submission, I go to my own Garden of Gethsemane to pray. I may not drip sweat like drops of blood, but I can tell you that my prayers there are agony. I don't want to get up until God has changed my heart so that I really mean it when I say, "Thy will be done."

After Jenni and I had been dating for a long time, she announced to me that she wasn't going to marry me after all. I was devastated. I didn't try to convince her to change her mind. I prayed like I'd never prayed before, but my prayer was about my relationship with God. I told him, "Lord, I submit myself to you. If she's not the one, so be it. I want to trust you. Right now, I'm struggling to accept your will, but I want you to work in me to soften my heart to you." It was like Jacob wrestling all night with the angel. I prayed and cried for four hours until I could say—and really mean, "Lord, I accept your will for my life."

As a wise, loving parent, God knows that for us to grow strong and mature, we have to learn some hard lessons to obey even when we don't want to obey and to wait when we want answers now. Thankfully, we don't come to these crisis points every day, but when they arise, we need to be ready. It's entirely normal for us to face them, wrestle with them and cry out to God for his mercy, and then choose to submit our hearts and our plans to him. It's not enough to obey on the outside but remain defiant inside. We need to go deep into the character of God, to experience his goodness and greatness more than ever before so that we gladly say, "Lord, not my will, but yours."

✚ **Read Acts 16:1-15.**

✚ **What are some differences between agreement and submission?**

✚ **Why is it not enough to obey on the outside but remain defiant on the inside? What are some consequences of inadequate submission?**

✚ **When was a time you needed to submit to the leading of God, a leader, a spouse, or the government? How did you do? How might you have responded better?**

✚ **Complete the following prayer: "Lord, there are times I really don't want to submit, but I need to learn to do it gladly. Help me to understand that you're the Lord and I'm not. Today, I want to…"**

DAY TWENTY-TWO
DISCERNMENT

"Once when we were going to
the place of prayer, we were met
by a slave girl who had a spirit by
which she predicted the future.
She earned a great deal of money
for her owners by fortune-telling. .
. . Finally Paul became so troubled
that he turned around and said to
the spirit, 'In the name of Jesus
Christ I command you to come out
of her!' At that moment the spirit
left her" (Acts 16:16, 18).

Through a vision and a boat ride, Paul, Silas, Timothy and Luke had made their way to Europe to tell people about Jesus. They met Lydia on a riverbank, and when they told her about Jesus, she trusted in Christ. She and her family were baptized, and she invited them to stay at her home.

As Luke tells us above, one day when Paul and his crew were on their way to the synagogue for prayer, they met a slave girl who was possessed by a demon. She had the supernatural ability to predict the future, and her owners made a killing when she put on a show. We might expect the demon to sound like the girl in The Exorcist, but instead, the girl's words seemed to affirm Paul and his message. Every time she saw them over the course of several days, she shouted, "These men are servants of the Most High God, who are telling you the way to be saved" (Acts 16:17).

Isn't that the gospel? Wasn't she speaking truth? I'm sure a lot of people felt that she had become Paul's partner, but he recognized a different spirit. Finally, he had enough. He spoke to the demon and commanded it to come out of her, and it left at that moment.

The concept of spiritual discernment is woven throughout the Bible. Solomon talks often in the Proverbs about the importance of this essential character quality. Years later, Paul writes the people in Philippi, "And this is my prayer: that your love may abound more and more in knowledge and depth of insight, so that you may be able to discern what is best and may be pure and blameless until the day of Christ, filled with the fruit of righteousness that comes through Jesus Christ—to the glory and praise of God" (Philippians 1:9-11). Paul explains to the Corinthians that spiritual discernment is essential if people want to understand the mysteries of God (1 Corinthians 2:14). In the same letter, he says that one of the gifts the Holy Spirit gives to members of the body of Christ is the ability to "distinguish between spirits" (1 Corinthians 12:10). And John reminds his readers that we must be disciplined and intentional to find out what's going on under the surface when people tell us they have spiritual truth. He wrote, "Dear friends, do not believe every spirit, but test the spirits to see whether they are from God, because many false prophets have gone out into the world" (1 John 4:1).

Perhaps the most common use of discernment is discovering God's will for our lives. When we first become believers, the choices are between good things and sinful things. The difference is often pretty clear. As we grow, however, we eliminate most of the gross, evil stuff out of our lives and begin to develop healthy, God-honoring patterns of life and relationships. Increasingly, the choices are between two equally good things, or maybe between a good thing and the best thing. That's why Paul prayed that God would enable the Philippians to discern what is "best."

For me, there are several elements in uncovering and following God's will. First, I have to want his will more than my own. Second, I ask God to clear away the distractions and conflicts in my mind so I can think clearly. I look for passages of Scripture that direct my thoughts and give me insight. Then, very simply, I ask God for wisdom about the choice. James tells us, "If any of you lacks wisdom, he should ask God, who gives generously to all without finding fault, and it will be given to him" (James 1:5). After I ask God, I listen carefully. Sometimes, an answer congeals in my mind right away, but often it takes days or even weeks. As I sense God's leading, I run it by some honest, wise, and trusted friends, including Jenni, who knows me better than anybody. They often give valuable input to craft the vision God has given me and provide insight about the direction and timing. But it's not over yet. The last element, one that determines the ultimate success of the venture, is the courage to take necessary steps to make it a reality. I can have a loaded cannon, but if I don't light the fuse, nothing will happen. I don't use this pattern of discerning God's will when I'm trying to decide between pepperoni or Italian sausage pizza, but I use it every time I face an important crossroads in my personal life, my most cherished relationships, or my leadership at the church.

Discernment enables us to tell truth from error, to uncover hidden motives, and to detect evil in people's hearts. When experts at the Treasury Department train bank tellers to spot counterfeit currency, they don't spend a lot of time pointing to the flaws in counterfeit bills. Instead, they focus almost entirely on the actual bills. They carefully examine the watermarks, the sheen of the ink, the details of the engraving, and all kinds of other features. When tellers become very familiar with the attributes of the real thing, they can easily spot any fakes. In the same way, Christians need to soak their minds and hearts in God's truth. The more we know the word of God and grasp the power of theological truth, the more easily we'll be able to spot errors when we read them or hear them. A friend of mine told me that a number of people in his church are teaching a new brand of spiritual healing for abuse victims. They claim Jesus will heal people "completely, instantaneously, and permanently" with a simple prayer. He told me, "People are flocking to these teachers because they're hearing things they really want to hear. They don't want to be taught that God uses pain as part of his process to deepen our faith. They just want relief, and they want it now!" Whenever I hear about a "new revelation," red lights start flashing in my heart.

We don't want to go around questioning everybody's motives. Being judgmental isn't a spiritual gift! But there are times when we're listening to someone talk about their work for God, and something in our spirits feels uncomfortable. They may be saying the right words, but we detect an undercurrent of arrogance and self-promotion. They love the limelight a little too much, or they're manipulating the situation to gain power and authority. The Scriptures tell us that humility is one of the most important, and maybe one of the most elusive, of character qualities in the lives of believers. We are naïve to think that anyone, including ourselves, has crystal clear motives. We are a mixed bag, and our hearts won't be completely pure until our old nature is gone when we see Christ in person. But for now, we can measure our hearts against the most powerful and accurate standard on earth: the Scriptures.

The writer to the Hebrews tells us, "For the word of God is living and active. Sharper than any double-edged sword, it penetrates even to dividing soul and spirit, joints and marrow; it judges the thoughts and attitudes of the heart. Nothing in all creation is hidden from God's sight. Everything is uncovered and laid bare before the eyes of him to whom we must give account" (Hebrews 4:12-13).

Too often, we give ourselves the benefit of the doubt, but we instantly assume the other person has evil, wicked motives. Before we become vigilantes to examine other people's motives, we first need to take a hard look at our own. If, though, we have prayed about our own motives and we detect an established pattern of selfish ambition in someone (not just a single instance), we can go to that person in love, not to judge but to restore, and share our observations and concerns. We shouldn't wait until it's become a huge deal to talk to someone we care about. It's much more productive and less threatening to come along side and say, "Hey, let me ask you about something. I may be wrong, but here's something I think I've seen in you over the past couple of weeks. Tell me what you're thinking." Sometimes, the person's explanation makes perfect sense, and we realize we misread the situation. Occasionally, the person says, "Oh my goodness, you're right. I've been calling attention to myself instead of God. Thank you for showing that to me." But sometimes, the person flares his nostrils in rage and attacks us, even if we've gone with humility and with several clear examples of the wrongs.

From time to time, we discern that a person is timid and lacks confidence. We can step into that person's life to speak words of hope and courage. I might say, "I see potential in you, and in fact, I see greatness. Let me help you find the best place for you." Almost always, a discerning word of kindness and targeted encouragement makes a big difference in that person's life. Parents need to be discerning about the needs and possibilities of their children. People in business need to listen to the Spirit and sometimes conclude, "I don't need to sign a contract with that guy. Something isn't right about him and his company."

Some time ago, I attended the newcomers' dinner at our church, and I met a couple I had never seen before. After talking to them only a couple of minutes, the Spirit of God whispered to me, "These guys are trouble. Watch out!"

I excused myself, and I walked over to our staff pastors. I told them, "Guys, keep an eye on that couple." I motioned to them and described them.

"They're here to cause a problem. I don't know what's going to happen, but I'm sure it's going to be ugly. I don't want them to have access to others in the room, so if you see them getting too close, move in and diplomatically change the subject in the conversation." The staff members looked only mildly surprised. They know that God gives insight, and they assumed he had given me discernment about the couple. They were ready.

When I spoke to the group, I told the story of the church, and I shared our vision for the community. I then handed the meeting over to Pastor Richard. I told everyone that I needed to leave so I could get to my small group. I explained, "Sorry, but small groups are a core value of our church, so I've got to go." Before the meeting was over, my father came to the membership dinner and met the couple. In a few minutes, he called the staff over and told them exactly what I'd said about them. The couple wasn't outwardly weird. They didn't have 666 written on their foreheads, and they didn't have Nazi Swastikas tattooed on their arms. Even though as a couple they looked very normal, the Spirit had warned both my father and me about them.

The next day, the couple came to my office. I had no idea why they had come. The look in their eye told me that they meant business, and this was going to be serious. The woman held out a handkerchief and showed me a part of a tooth. She said she had broken it on the chicken at the dinner last night. I knew that was a lie. Her husband burst into the conversation, "If you don't pay us one thousand dollars we'll file a lawsuit against the church."

I refused to pay them a cent, and after threatening me several more times, they left my office. When I talked to some other pastors in the area, I learned that they had tried the same trick on them. To be honest, I'm a pretty soft touch. If God hadn't warned me about them, I'd have gladly given them money, provided a dentist, and done everything possible to make it right. The Lord's whisper saved us a lot of money and taught us a big lesson about listening to the Spirit.

I've talked to men who tried to convince me that God had led them into intimate relationships with married women. I've had to confront people who smiled sweetly as they lied through their teeth. I've had to figure out if a person's arrogant attitude was blatant self-righteousness or a mask to cover up deep insecurities. If we're left to our own abilities, we won't detect many secrets in the lives of people around us. Discernment is a spiritual gift for a few believers, but all of us can listen to the Spirit's whisper and have more spiritual insight. It's normal for him to give us discernment about the Father's will, truth and error, uncover hidden motives, and detect the presence of evil. Are you listening?

✝ **Read Acts 16:16-18.**

✝ **What difference would it make in your life if you use the elements of discerning God's will in today's lesson?**

✝ **When is it appropriate and when is it foolish to question someone's motives?**

✝ **What is the role of the Scriptures in discernment? What are some reasons you need to tap into biblical truth so that it guides your thinking and observations?**

✝ **Complete the following prayer: "Jesus, I want to sharpen my discernment. Make me a good listener, and give me insight. Today, I need it for…"**

DAY TWENTY-THREE
THE POWER OF GRATITUDE

> "About midnight Paul and Silas were praying and singing hymns to God, and the other prisoners were listening to them. Suddenly there was such a violent earthquake that the foundations of the prison were shaken. At once all the prison doors flew open, and everybody's chains came loose" (Acts 16:25-26).

When we love God with all our hearts and take risks to obey him no matter what, we don't use our faith and obedience as leverage to get God to make our lives successful and happy. Jesus loved the Father and obeyed every moment of every day, and the Father led him through countless difficulties, and eventually, to the cross. In the next scene in Luke's history of the early church, we find out what happened after Paul cast the demon out of the slave girl. She was free from the demonic presence, but Paul's faithful actions had cost him his freedom. Paul and his companion Silas, however, didn't wallow in self-pity when things didn't go the way they hoped. They still trusted God and poured out their love for him in songs of gratitude. But before we witness their faith, we need to understand the situation.

The fortunetelling slave girl had made her owners a pile of money, but when Paul cast out the demon, their source of revenue was gone. They must have led a mob against the two evangelists. They grabbed Paul and Silas, took them to the magistrates, and accused them of treason against Rome. The crowd, always looking for a good fight, joined in the attack. The magistrates were satisfied that the two men were, indeed, troublemakers, so he ordered that they to be stripped and beaten with rods—long, whip-like pieces of wood that gained momentum when they were swung, much like a golf club in the hands of a good golfer. The power of each blow was damaging and painful. After the men were beaten to a pulp, the jailer put them in the deepest, darkest, most forbidding part of the dungeon and fastened their feet in stocks.

I can imagine being in that condition: bleeding and broken from the rods, half-naked, falsely accused, immobile and sitting on the damp floor, with very little light. I would have thought about the vision God had given us that brought us to Philippi, and I might have wondered, "What in the world is going on? All this must be a huge mistake? Where is God, anyway?" But Paul and Silas didn't have a complaining heart, and they weren't consumed with self-pity. Instead, in the silence and darkness of the dungeon, they prayed out loud and sang hymns of praise to God.

As they sang, a violent earthquake shook the prison. The cell doors flew open and the prisoners' chains fell off. The jailer understood the seriousness of the circumstances. Like Japanese officers many centuries later who committed hara kiri when they had failed their emperor, the jailer took up his sword to commit suicide because he had failed to keep the prisoners confined. The prisoners, though, hadn't left the building. In the darkness, Paul yelled to him, "Don't harm yourself! We are all here!" (Acts 16:28).

In a remarkable turn of events, "The jailer called for lights, rushed in and fell trembling before Paul and Silas. He then brought them out and asked, 'Sirs, what must I do to be saved?' " (Acts 16:29-30) I guess he'd been listening to their prayers and songs.

The jailer must have taken Paul and Silas to the quarters where his family lived because Luke tells us that the two men shared the gospel with the jailer and his family. As a result, the whole family believed in Christ, and Paul and Silas baptized them in the middle of the night. The jailer washed the two men's wounds, and presumably, found them something to wear. Luke describes the event, "The jailer brought them into his house and set a meal before them; he was filled with joy because he had come to believe in God—he and his whole family" (Acts 16:34).

The next part of the story is pretty funny. The magistrates who had ordered the men to be beaten and jailed must have had a change of heart. They sent orders for the jailer to release Paul and Silas and demanded they leave the city, but the two men refused to leave. Their purpose was to plant a church in that city, and they knew that if they weren't completely exonerated of the accusations, there would be a cloud of suspicion over the church for many years. Paul told them, "They beat us publicly without a trial, even though we are Roman citizens, and threw us into prison. And now do they want to get rid of us quietly? No! Let them come themselves and escort us out" (Acts 16:37).

Roman citizens! Oops. It was illegal for the magistrates to order any Roman citizen to be beaten, especially without a formal trial, which, of course, they hadn't received. The tables had turned in the city. The magistrates apologized profusely, and they escorted them out of the prison. Paul and Silas met with the other believers at Lydia's house, and soon left to talk about Jesus in another town.

The focal point of this story is the time when Paul and Silas were in the deepest part of the prison. They were low geographically, but not spiritually. Even though things hadn't gone the way they hoped, they didn't give up on God or his purposes for them. The greatness of God—his love, mercy, and mysterious ways—superceded the magnitude of their problems. No matter what, they held on to God's glory and grace, so instead of complaining or plotting some kind of escape, they spent their time praying (for the jailer's salvation, I'd assume) and singing praises to God. Every prisoner heard them in the stillness of the night. I can imagine that some of them became believers and were the people sitting in the church who heard Paul's letter read to them some years later.

The attacks, arrest, beatings, and jail, weren't obstacles to God's plan. Somehow, God used them as part of his design to accomplish his purposes. When we realize that problems are part of God's purposes, we'll sing instead of griping. It's not about our comfort; it's about God's glory. Paul and Silas were convinced that God's ways may be mysterious, but his will is always good and right and pure. With strong faith in his character, they didn't have to understand the details of what he was doing.

Why did Paul and Silas sing that night? Did they think God would honor their faith by sending an earthquake? Did they sing and pray as a strategy for escape? Certainly not, they sang only to express their love for God and their trust in him, expecting that God would give them strength to face anything that might appear on the horizon. They were like the three men centuries before who faced the furnace with strong faith. Daniel tells us the king threatened them with incineration if they didn't renounce God. Their response is a model of openhanded faith: "Shadrach, Meshach and Abednego replied to the king, 'O Nebuchadnezzar, we do not need to defend ourselves before you in this matter. If we are thrown into the blazing furnace, the God we serve is able to save us from it, and he will rescue us from your hand, O king. But even if he does not, we want you to know, O king, that we will not serve your gods or worship the image of gold you have set up' " (Daniel 3:16-18).

When things don't go the way we want them to go—especially when we've followed Christ with all our hearts—how do we respond? Do we stand firm in our faith in God's character, or do we let the problems we're facing blot out the sunlight of God's glory and purposes for us? We're not invincible, and we're not all-knowing. We are flawed, finite human beings who can't possibly understand all that the Almighty God of the universe is doing. Paul later explained his humble, but faith-filled, perspective this way: "But we have this treasure in jars of clay to show that this all-surpassing power is from God and not from us. We are hard pressed on every side, but not crushed; perplexed, but not in despair; persecuted, but not abandoned; struck down, but not destroyed. We always carry around in our body the death of Jesus, so that the life of Jesus may also be revealed in our body" (2 Corinthians 4:7-10). When we have this perspective, we're willing to die to our own expectations and demands every day so that the love and life of Jesus can shine out from us.

We can pray and praise even when we're confused and hurting. We don't have to wait until we have all the answers and it feels great to honor him with our attitudes. God delights in his children expressing their loyalty and love in spite of their fears and doubts. And as we exercise the sacrifice of praise, God works in our hearts to change us. Gradually, as our minds are focused on God's goodness and glory, instead of our problems, we relax in his strong hands, and we trust him more. Then, the words of praise we spoke as a spiritual discipline become heartfelt joy. The transformation may not happen in a few minutes or a few days, but it can happen. Praise may begin as a tenacious choice, but it results in genuine gladness and renewed faith. The ultimate trust is to believe God is more real than our circumstances. Even in suffering, loss, and death, we can sing praises to him, not because we're comfortable but because he's God. And sometimes, he causes earthquakes.

Our family has seen the power of praise in a seemingly hopeless circumstance. I'll let my mother tell the story:

It was April 18, 1971, and our beautiful son, Brent, had arrived! He was a good baby, happy and content. However, he had digestion and breathing problems from birth, which meant we spent a lot of time at the doctors' offices. After many tests, we were told that Brent had cystic fibrosis (CF). His life span was estimated at three to five years of age.

This disease is a genetic disorder that must be carried in the genes of both parents. I had two brothers and a sister die from breathing and digestion conditions. Tom's (my husband) side of the family also carried the CF gene. Three of his paternal cousins were diagnosed in the Children's Medical Center at Parkland Hospital, Dallas, Texas, and the noted physician and the head of the Cystic Fibrosis Foundation of Texas, who also was Brent's physician, treated them. All three of Tom's cousins succumbed to the disease at a young age.

After being in and out of the Children's Medical Center of Dallas over a period of fifteen months, Brent was again back in the hospital for two weeks of tests and treatment. A rigorous treatment regimen was to begin the following week on Monday, and we wanted Brent home for the weekend before he became weaker.

Brent could not be in a crowd, because his weakened immune system made him susceptible to any germ or disease carried by others. We took him to church with us on Sunday night to Calvary Temple in Mesquite, Texas, where my husband was pastor. My mother-in-law kept him in Tom's office to protect him from the crowd, and was able to listen to the service by speakers installed in the office.

That Sunday we had a choir in concert at our church from a neighboring African American congregation. Wow! They sang with great freedom and joy. One song, "I Know Who Holds Tomorrow," was sung. The choir director sensed the song was conveying a powerful message to the crowd so they sang the verse, and then repeated the chorus about a dozen times!

The verse reads:

"I don't know about tomorrow, I just live from day to day;
I don't borrow from its sunshine, for its skies may turn to gray;
I don't worry o'er the future, for I know what Jesus said,
And today I'll walk beside Him, for He knows what is ahead."

And the chorus:

"Many things about tomorrow, I don't seem to understand;
But I know who holds tomorrow, and I know who holds my hand!"

As our faith began to build, my husband said, "Brenda, go back to the office and get Brent and bring him out here. As of this night, Brent is healed." Tom walked to the platform with Brent in his arms, held him up before our church congregation, and said, "Look at Brent's frail body. This will be the last time you see him like this. God has healed him."

Brent started improving immediately. We went back to the Children's Medical Center of Dallas for treatment. The "Salt Test" is the diagnostic test indicating the presence of CF. After several weeks, we asked the doctor for another diagnostic test. He reluctantly agreed, because he was sure of the previous diagnosis. The Salt Test came back negative. Brent was healed.

The prominent physician asked to meet with us in his office. He questioned us as to what we had done at home for Brent. We told him that we had prayed asking Jesus to heal him. We had taken him to a church meeting, and during the service believed he was healed and announced it to the congregation.

The doctor said, "There are so many children I could help if I knew what made him well. Please tell what you have done differently." We again repeated, "We prayed, and God healed him!" The physician (who had treated Tom's three cousins who died from CF) said, "Well, besides that," and then exclaimed, "If Brent is healed, I've healed him!"

Brent was the healthiest of our four sons after his healing. He did not have the usual childhood illnesses that generally occur. Thirty-eight years later, Brent is still well and very healthy. When God does something, he does it well!

It's normal to experience pain, suffering, and times of confusion as we walk with God, but as we face hard times, we can look beyond the difficult situation into the loving, patient, and wise face of God. No matter what, we can make the choice to pray and praise. And sometimes, God causes earthquakes.

✤ Read Acts 16:19-40.

✤ We aren't usually surprised when we suffer because we've sinned. Why are we often surprised (and dismayed) when we suffer as a result of obeying God?

✤ Why do you think God might take great delight in his children praying and praising as a discipline even when they don't feel like it? What are some positive results this discipline produces in us?

✤ When have you found yourself in a dungeon, beaten, misunderstood, and alone? How did you respond? How would it have changed you, if not the situation, if you had focused on prayer and praise during that time?

✤ Complete the following prayer: "Lord Jesus, you are worthy of my praise in the good times and the bad, simply because you're God. Today, I want to make the choice to praise you no matter what. Help me to…"

DAY TWENTY-FOUR
STRATEGY & TENACITY

"When the Jews in Thessalonica learned that Paul was preaching the word of God at Berea, they went there too, agitating the crowds and stirring them up. The brothers immediately sent Paul to the coast, but Silas and Timothy stayed at Berea. The men who escorted Paul brought him to Athens and then left with instructions for Silas and Timothy to join him as soon as possible"
(Acts 17:13-15).

There was a Christian who had a certain way of sharing his faith with homeless people that endured a lot of criticism from others in his church. In response he would simply smile and tell them, without a bit of anger, "I can see your point. I'm always open to learning new and more effective ways of sharing my faith. So, how do you tell these people about Christ?" He would wait a few seconds, but no one ever answered him. Finally, he would say, "I see. Well, I like the way I tell them about Jesus better than the way you don't tell them. I think I'll stick with what I'm doing."

If we're serious about reaching lost people, God will weave together our past experiences, personal testimony, hobbies and interests, intellect, and personalities to construct a strategy we can use to tell people about Christ. As we practice and try new ways of communicating with people, we'll find that some things we do work better than others. A friend of mine had been sharing his faith for many years, and his church asked him to teach a class on evangelism. One Saturday, he took one of the students out to visit people and practice what they had been learning. My friend told me, "I'd been doing evangelism for a long time, and as the teacher, I planned to show this young man how to do it. I shared the gospel with the first person we met as a follow up from the church visitor list, and it went fine. When we got to the next house, I said, 'This time, you share and I'll watch.' As he talked, I've never heard a more beautiful and powerful gospel presentation in my life! The man and his wife came to Christ, and I was so moved by the power of his message that I fell in love with Christ more than ever. I realized that an old dog like me could learn a few new tricks."

Paul developed a very clear strategy to reach people in every city. Jesus had given him the mission of reaching Gentiles, but he knew that the Jews already knew a lot about God and the promised Messiah. If some of them believed, they'd become leaders of the new churches and reach out to the Gentiles. Even when the Jews attacked him, Paul didn't deviate from his strategy.

When Paul and Silas left Philippi, they traveled to Thessalonica and spoke out about Christ in the synagogue. As it happened in city after city, some believed, some doubted, and some became furious with them. Jewish leaders were jealous of their popularity, and they incited a mob to start a riot. They searched for Paul and Silas, but when they couldn't be found, the mob dragged Jason, a new convert, in front of the city officials to accuse him. Again, the charge wasn't loitering or jaywalking; it was treason, proclaiming another king besides Caesar.

Under cover of night, Paul and Silas slipped out of town and went to Berea. When they spoke in the synagogue there, a strange thing happened: the people decided to read the Scriptures carefully to see if what they were saying was true. They discovered that Paul and Silas were speaking accurately about God's provision of a suffering Messiah and the resurrection from the dead, so "many of the Jews believed, as did also a number of the prominent Greek women and many Greek men" (Acts 17:12). Trouble, however, always dogged their steps. Some of the angry mob from Thessalonica heard they were preaching in Berea, and came to attack them there. Again, Paul and Silas had to flee for their lives, but Timothy stayed in Berea to help the new church grow strong.

They traveled to Athens. Again, they preached in the synagogue, however they knew the real power of influence in that culture was held by the philosophers who hung out in the marketplace and on the hill above it. To connect the message of Christ with them, Paul took a different tack. He began by affirming their thirst for God. He then pointed to an idol with the inscription: "To an unknown God." From that point, he explained that Jesus was the God who had been unknown to them, but far from remaining a mystery, he had revealed himself in nature, the incarnation, the cross, and the resurrection. Again, a few people grasped God's grace and became the nucleus for a church plant in Athens.

Sometimes I hear people say, "We need to be like the church in Acts." I almost laugh. I want to respond, "Okay, great. We'll first go to the synagogue, and then we'll face a riot of furious, jealous people who hate our guts. A few people will believe, and that will be our church—forged in the fires of opposition. Is that what you're looking for?" No, probably not, at least not in America. Christians in China, Myanmar, Nepal, parts of India, and Islamic countries face the kind of opposition that the disciples endured in Acts, but we enjoy tremendous freedom and protection. The question is this: What will we do with the opportunities we've been given?

Jesus often used agrarian metaphors to communicate spiritual truth. Many of his parables were about wheat and weeds, sowing and reaping, hard ground and fertile soil. When we sow seeds of the gospel, we can expect a wide range of responses, just like the reactions to Jesus, Paul, and believers throughout the ages. God has made some of us gifted at sowing, and some at harvesting. It doesn't mean that one is superior to the other. We're all working for the same purpose in the same big field. I've heard it said that it takes at least six gospel presentations for someone to believe, some more and some fewer. In their insightful book, What's Gone Wrong with the Harvest?, James Engel and Wilbert Norton identify a scale which depicts an individual's growing responsiveness to the gospel, from awareness of the supernatural, to awareness of the facts of the gospel, to awareness of one's personal need for salvation, and finally to repentance and faith.

Our task when we talk to people isn't to twist their arms and force them to pray the sinner's prayer. We must also remember that we're not failures if they say, "Thanks, but it's not for me." Our task is to share the message as clearly as possible, as lovingly as possible, in the power of the Spirit, and leave the results to God. If God uses us to move the person one notch up the awareness scale, it's been a successful meeting. And even if we see no movement at all, as long as we've been faithful we should feel great about our attempt to share the good news.

I love to hear about the creative ways people talk to others about Jesus. Their strategies range from simple to complex, from personal to high tech. They use their God-given strengths and experiences to connect with people in their spheres of influence. I know men and women involved in motorcycle clubs who often tell people at rest stops, restaurants, and gatherings like Sturgis about Jesus. My friend Anthony in Austin hosts poker tournaments in his home and invites people from the neighborhood to play. Many of these people would never come to church, but they hear about Christ as they play Texas Hold 'Em. Another friend has led ten men to Christ after inviting them to come to his home and watch Ultimate Fighting Championship bouts. He buys chicken wings, invites guys in his small group to join them, and after the match is over, they talk about what's meaningful in their lives. Inevitably, Jesus becomes a big topic of discussion. Another guy takes men fishing, and while they're out in his boat, he talks to them about Christ's love. Dr. Hugh Ross is an astronomer who founded the ministry Reasons to Believe. He uses the platform of God's magnificent creation to share the gospel with people. Scientists and engineers who don't think Christians ever use their brains are drawn to his rich science and deep faith.

Some of you are thinking, "Yeah, but it's not right to go to bars, play poker, watch violence, or glorify science. We just need to tell people to come to church." But the people whose lives are being touched at these events and in these ways wouldn't come to church. These bold, compassionate evangelists are going where the lost are. Jesus caught flack for going to Samaria and talking to a woman who had five husbands. My friends are just doing what Jesus modeled. They're going where lost people are, connecting with them, and faithfully presenting the gospel of Christ.

As we're involved in various kinds of events that build relationships with others, we need to remember why we're there. For Jesus, it wasn't about getting a drink of water; it was about reaching a woman's heart. For Paul, it wasn't about philosophy or power; it was about finding men and women whose hearts were open. For us, it's not about fishing, softball, poker, flowers, flying, fights, or anything like that; it's about sharing the gospel of forgiveness with people who desperately need a Savior. Jesus said that we're the salt of the earth, but he warned, "Salt is good, but if it loses its saltiness, how can it be made salty again? It is fit neither for the soil nor for the manure pile; it is thrown out" (Luke 14:34-35). Some of us think that we're only salty if we're using a King James Bible and commanding people to be holy. Jesus didn't do anything like that. He went where people were, talked their language, and imparted both grace and truth to them. Because he loved them, many responded in faith. If people know we love them, they're much more likely to open their ears and their hearts to our words about Jesus. Love and truth are both essential ingredients in spiritual salt.

An incarnational lifestyle means that we embody the life and heart of Jesus. In the same way he touched people in his day, we touch them today. For us, it's completely normal to examine our lives to see what connection points God has built between us and others. Our interests, education, and background aren't an accident. God wants us to use them to build bridges with people around us. God has carefully crafted and equipped each of us to reach people, and we are very different. There are people I can reach that you can't reach, but there are people who will respond to you who wouldn't respond to me. God sovereignly puts us where he wants us to shine as lights and be salty to make people thirsty for him. It's no accident we're in our neighborhoods, schools and offices. God has put us in these locations for a reason. We need to celebrate our differences instead of criticizing each other for having unique methods of evangelism.

When God leads us to invest our 50 hours, we may end up working on any type of project—helping people move, building a playground for kids, caring for the elderly, and hundreds of other important things to serve people. In all of those, we need to remember that we're light and salt. It's a normal part of who we are. Loving and serving others is integrated into the fabric of our daily lives.

✥ **Read Acts 17:34.**

✥ **Describe Paul's strategy to tell people about Jesus. Describe Jesus' strategy.**

✥ **What are your interests, education, and background that enable you to connect with certain people in your world? How does (or might) God use those to help you build bridges with people around you?**

✥ **Who are two or three unbelievers in your life you'd like to tell about Jesus? What are the common connection points between you? How will you bring up the topic of faith?**

✥ **Complete the following prayer: "Jesus, you didn't stand back and wait for people to come to you. You took the initiative to go to them, and you came to me, too. Please use me in these people's lives…"**

DAY TWENTY-FIVE
DON'T BE AFRAID

> "One night the Lord spoke to Paul in a vision: 'Do not be afraid; keep on speaking, do not be silent. For I am with you, and no one is going to attack and harm you, because I have many people in this city.' So Paul stayed for a year and a half, teaching them the word of God" (Acts 18:9-11).

After Paul left Athens, he traveled west to the city of Corinth where he met a couple, Aquila and Priscilla, who had fled Rome because the emperor ordered all the Jews to leave. In Corinth, Paul needed money, so he worked as a tentmaker for a while until Silas and Timothy joined him. Every Sabbath, he spoke in the local synagogue about Jesus. The Jews again attacked him (I think there's a pattern here!), so he went next door and established a church in the home of Titius Justus. One of the new believers was Crispus, an official in the synagogue. Crispus' whole family, as well as "many Corinthians," believed in Jesus and were baptized.

Luke doesn't tell us what was going on in Paul's mind and heart during this time, but we can make the assumption that the threats, beatings, and ridicule were taking their toll on the stalwart leader of the new faith. As we've seen repeatedly throughout Luke's history, following Jesus never guarantees an easy life. Following Jesus is the most exciting adventure the world has ever known, but it carries inherent risks. The timid need not apply. The man who faced fierce opposition in every city, preached the word with boldness and kindness, and witnessed God work miracles in every city he visited . . . this man needed some encouragement from God. Luke tells us, "One night the Lord spoke to Paul in a vision: 'Do not be afraid; keep on speaking, do not be silent. For I am with you, and no one is going to attack and harm you, because I have many people in this city' " (Acts 18:9-10).

All of us need a word of encouragement from time to time. Giving, loving, and serving is fun and refreshing a lot of the time, but it can become a grind; especially when we feel alone or when we're not seeing as much fruit as we hoped to see. In times of discouragement, God may give us a vision like he gave Paul, but far more often, the word comes from a trusted friend who looks into our eyes, sees the expression of exhaustion or hopelessness, and speaks a strong word of peace, hope, and love to our hearts. When Paul was in Corinth, God pulled out the stops to encourage his lion of the faith. God gave Paul a vision, and he brought good friends—Silas, Timothy, Aquila, Priscilla, and Apollos—to stand by him. Paul found the strength to keep going from these sources.

It might be a lot easier if the Christian life were simply a checklist of activities that we had to accomplish before we die. We wouldn't have to put our hearts into what we were doing, we wouldn't have to pursue God in order to transform our hearts, and the needs and wounds of others around us wouldn't bother us, nor would we care that much about the eternal destiny of those around us. The normal Christian life, however, isn't a bunch of boxes for us to check off. It's a vital relationship with the God of the universe.

In city after city, Paul not only proclaimed the message of Christ, he embodied the character, love and strength of Christ. Paul stayed in Corinth for a year and a half and while he was there, God changed people's lives, and many were attracted to the reality of Christ in the daily experience of believers. Friedrich Nietzsche, one of the foremost atheists of the nineteenth century, once commented, "These people must show me they are redeemed before I will believe in their redeemer." The lives of many believers, it's sad to say, do not demonstrate much redemption. We are just as selfish as unbelievers, just as impatient when we wait in lines, just as resentful when we don't get our way, and just as angry when we express our opinions. Well, that's not quite true. A study conducted years ago by Josh McDowell showed that Christian's drink, commit adultery, use drugs, and engage in blatant sins of the flesh only ten percent less than the population of non-Christians. My friend, that's not the normal Christian life! But I'm not suggesting that avoiding these sins is the benchmark of righteousness, nor that by not engaging in these sins we're somehow fine with God. God wants far more than our adherence to a list of restricted behaviors—he wants our hearts.

After Paul left Corinth, he later wrote them a long letter to remind them of the things he had taught. In it, he addressed their propensity to engage in sexual sins. Instead of just telling the Corinthians, "Don't do it!" Paul told them that they needed to remember that their identities had changed. They weren't the same people they used to be. Our choices are a reflection of our view of God and of ourselves as his beloved children. Paul wrote, "Flee from sexual immorality. All other sins a man commits are outside his body, but he who sins sexually sins against his own body. Do you not know that your body is a temple of the Holy Spirit, who is in you, whom you have received from God? You are not your own; you were bought at a price. Therefore honor God with your body" (1 Corinthians 6:18-20).

Corinth was a city of blatant, unbridled sin. One of the problems in the church at Corinth was that men visited the temple prostitutes. Some would say it's not that much different for some men today—they just go to different buildings to hang out in topless bars or view pornography. But when God transforms a group of people, they have an impact in every aspect of the community's culture. In the eighteenth century, the Great Awakening swept across the colonies in America. Some of the greatest preachers the world has ever known were active in those days, including Jonathan Edwards, John Wesley, and George Whitefield. On one occasion, Whitefield commented, "Thus when the apostolic church declared the hour cometh and now is, this is the age of the Spirit. The church itself and its total life was part of the dramatic truth. For men encountering that church felt—even though they were pagans, a waft of the supernatural—a mysterious power like the stirring of the dawn wind."

Too often, we live with a misconception of the Christian life. Some of us are on the side of Christian liberty, and we attack people who are too rigid, legalistic, and judgmental. Those of us who value righteousness and following God's commands look at our more free-spirited brothers and sisters and shake our heads in disgust. The question isn't which one is right and which is wrong, that only leads to deeper divisions. Nor is the answer to find an elusive "balance" between the law and license. There's a third way, the one Jesus lived and Paul preached and modeled—that is, a genuine experience of the grace of God which fills us with love and life so that we long to please the one who bought us. Our identity has changed because we are now "in Christ." We're no longer free-spirited people who let it all hang out to prove we live by grace, and we're no longer angry, superior, law-loving people who find sport in condemning people who don't follow the rules as closely as we do.

When we are finally gripped by grace, we realize we are fallen and flawed, but redeemed by the love of God. Our reason to live isn't to find more freedom but to honor and obey the one who loves us so much. And when we are filled with his grace and love, we realize that none of us meets his perfect standard. There's no room for feeling judgmental or superior, but in humility we love one another. That's what was so attractive about the family of God in the first century, and it's no different today. People can't wait to come to a church, or join a group, where God's amazing grace is changing lives. God transforms our hearts and desires so that we no longer obey because we have to, but because we want to.

Does this kind of life sound attractive to you? It does to me! But it's risky. It requires me to be ruthlessly honest about my faults and flaws, to realize when I'm selfish or prideful, and when I face temptations of any kind. I have to practice repentance as a lifestyle, trusting God to cleanse me, renew me, and give me the power to change. I can't change myself at the deepest level where change is necessary. I have to trust in the power of the Holy Spirit to transform me from the inside out.

When people rejected Paul's message about Christ, it broke his heart, just as it did Jesus when he wept over Jerusalem because the people didn't believe in him. Paul cried out for his Jewish family to respond in faith to the Messiah who loved them and died for them. Though Paul left the synagogues in each city when the Jews rejected him and began to abuse him, he never gave up on his countrymen. He kept going back to the Jews in every town to tell them that their long-awaited Messiah had come at last. However, he always took the message of grace to the broader audience of the Gentiles. In every city and in every site, some people hardened their hearts and some believed. Unfortunately, we see the same responses today.

We find an amusing side note in Luke's account of Paul's stay in Corinth. After Paul had been there for a long time, another dispute arose about him. The Jews dragged Paul into court and accused him of "persuading people to worship God in ways contrary to the law" (Acts 18:13). The judge threw out the charge, and the Jews got so angry they "turned on Sosthenes, the synagogue ruler, and beat him in front of the court" (Acts 18:17). Many years later when Paul wrote back to the Christians in Corinth, he mentioned a friend in the letter who was with him. This friend had become so close that Paul listed him as a co-author of the letter. The first line reads, "Paul, called to be an apostle of Christ Jesus by the will of God, and our brother Sosthenes . . ." Sosthenes may have been beaten to a pulp, but he became a believer and another source of encouragement to Paul. I think that's pretty cool.

Compassion makes us vulnerable. We can hide behind masks of success, pleasure, and approval, and we can play games with our Christian faith, making it only a "show without substance." But when our hearts break because people don't respond to the love of Christ, we become fragile, wounded, and afraid. If it could happen to Paul, it can certainly happen to you and me. As we invest hours in serving people, most of the people we help will be thrilled. A few, however, will question our motives or ridicule us in some way. When we experience compassion fatigue, we need to look for a word of encouragement from God. He'll bring it, sometimes from a source we wouldn't expect, like a vision in the night, but he'll bring it.

A couple of years ago when I traveled to Belarus on a mission trip, I was excited to go and tell people about Christ. I asked my friend Ken Marks to go along, but I had no idea how much I'd need him. When we arrived, one of the leaders there told me that none of what I planned to teach would work in their culture. In addition, the communist government was out to get us. My excitement quickly evaporated into a cloud of anxiety, but Ken was a lifesaver. His calm, strong faith and constant encouragement kept me going when I might have bailed out. We were like the Skipper and Gilligan. Ken is bigger than me, and he often told me, "I'm looking out for you, little buddy." I'll never forget our time together.

When God puts someone on our hearts to speak words of affirmation and hope, we need to pay attention instead of assuming they will just think we're weird. And when God sends someone to give us a word of encouragement, we need to accept it as God's message from his heart to ours. We are part of one body and one family with one hope and one heart. We need one another to keep going when we get discouraged. When God puts a friend, spouse, child, or leader on your heart, speak up. And when someone speaks to you, embrace the message. We need each other—that's normal. No one, not even Paul, is above the need for encouragement.

✛ Read Acts 18:1-28.

✛ Why do you think Paul may have been afraid? Are you surprised by this emotion in him? Why or why not?

✛ What are some ways God might bring a word of encouragement to a tired and fearful person who is faithfully serving him?

✛ Instead of law or license, how would you describe "the third way" to live?

✛ Complete the following prayer: "Lord Jesus, I'm sometimes tired and afraid, and I need a word of encouragement. Thank you for reminding me that I'm never alone. Today, I want to remember…"

DAY TWENTY-SIX
TRUE REPENTANCE

"When this became known to the Jews and Greeks living in Ephesus, they were all seized with fear, and the name of the Lord Jesus was held in high honor. Many of those who believed now came and openly confessed their evil deeds. A number who had practiced sorcery brought their scrolls together and burned them publicly. When they calculated the value of the scrolls, the total came to fifty thousand drachmas. In this way the word of the Lord spread widely and grew in power"
(Acts 19:17-20).

Repentance means to turn. Spiritually, it refers to turning away from sin and choosing to follow God and his directives. When Paul left Corinth, he walked across the country, up to the opening of the Black Sea, then down the coast of modern day Turkey to the metropolis of Ephesus, one of the greatest and richest cities of the world at that time. When he arrived, he met twelve people who had heard only a partial message about Christ, but they had believed everything they heard. They said they had received John's baptism, perhaps from John himself years earlier at the Jordan, or maybe from Apollos before he met Paul and understood the gospel more clearly. When Paul placed his hands on these eager disciples, they were filled with the Holy Spirit, and they spoke in tongues and prophesied (Acts 19:6).

According to his usual strategy, Paul spoke out boldly in the synagogue for three months. When he received fierce opposition, Paul moved his classes to the lecture hall of Tyrannus, where he taught every day. His message transformed lives and Luke tells us, "This went on for two years, so that all the Jews and Greeks who lived in the province of Asia heard the word of the Lord" (Acts 19:10). Why were people so interested? Because the power of God was clearly on display, changing lives. "God did extraordinary miracles through Paul, so that even handkerchiefs and aprons that had touched him were taken to the sick, and their illnesses were cured and the evil spirits left them" (Acts 19:11-12).

During this time of extraordinary work by the Spirit, Luke records an interesting encounter between a demon-possessed man and some Jews who were obviously jealous of Paul's anointing. They tried to use the name of Jesus to cast out demons just like they had seen Paul do on several occasions. One day, a demon responded to them, "Jesus I know, and I know about Paul, but who are you?" The man who was possessed by the demon attacked them and beat them to a pulp! "They ran out of the house naked and bleeding" (Acts 19:15-16).

Ephesus was home to a large number of spiritualists and magicians. They made their living by telling fortunes and conjuring spells. When these people saw the power of the Holy Spirit to heal, forgive, and save, they became terrified. They realized that all of their magic arts were worthless; the only one worth following was Jesus Christ. Luke tells us about an amazing event: "Many of those who believed now came and openly confessed their evil deeds. A number who had practiced sorcery brought their scrolls together and burned them publicly" (Acts 19:18-19). The scrolls weren't just a collection of books. The value, of their magic formulas and secrets was roughly eight million dollars in today's money. Burning them showed that this was a genuine awakening. The name of Christ was honored, the power of the Spirit worked miracles, and many people repented publicly of their sins. In Ephesus, the idol manufacturers lost a lot of business when the people turned to Christ. They became so angry that they started a riot. Now that's an amazing result of a community-wide revival!

Some of us have the wrong idea about repenting of our sins. We think of sins as a list of do's and don'ts, and we see God as an angry judge or disapproving grade school teacher. Our motivation to avoid sin, then, is only to get out of any punishment. Instead of longing for righteousness, we spend our time trying not to get caught! Forgiveness wipes the slate clean, but it doesn't take the permanent frown off the face of the judge or teacher. We live under a cloud of fear and doubt.

The Scriptures, though, give a very different picture of repentance, one that can revolutionize a person's relationship with God. We read over and over again in the Bible that God loves us, which should not be understood as an academic statement. It means that he cares deeply about our welfare, he wants to have a rich, real relationship with us, and he wants us to love him back. When we sin, we're not just breaking a commandment, we're breaking his heart. In his letter to the Ephesians, Paul tells us not to "grieve" the Spirit. This means that we, as finite human beings, have the power to make the infinite God sad. This concept is all too familiar to every parent reading these words. We long to have a loving, affirming, respectful, open relationship with our kids. When we have those times of warm and positive communication, our hearts sing! But when our children defy us, resent us when we're trying to guide them, or stomp their feet and walk away, it breaks our hearts. That's exactly how God feels when we ignore, defy, resent, or openly flaunt his kindness in an arrogant way.

Paul explains that there are two kinds of repentance—one based on a concept of an angry God, and the other on the idea of God's love and sadness. His first letter to the Corinthians pointed out several areas in which change was needed. Later, he received a message that they had taken his correction to heart. He wrote back, "Now I am happy, not because you were made sorry, but because your sorrow led you to repentance. For you became sorrowful as God intended and so were not harmed in any way by us. Godly sorrow brings repentance that leads to salvation and leaves no regret, but worldly sorrow brings death" (2 Corinthians 7:9-10).

Do you see the difference? The sorrow God intends doesn't crush us. It reminds us of his love, points us in a healthy direction, and restores our relationship with him—that's a "salvation that leaves no regret"! We feel genuinely sorry for our sins, not just because we got caught or feel sure we're going to get punished, but because we realize we've made someone who loves us very sad. The other kind of sorrow is shame. It pulverizes us into the dust, telling us that we're scum and that we'll never measure up no matter how hard we try. This kind of sorrow leaves us hopeless and full of anger. Many people who endure this sorrow eventually become depressed—a kind of death of the soul.

Repentance also involves a change of behavior. The transformation always correlates with the specific sin in the person's life. For instance, the magicians in Ephesus burned their scrolls, which were central to their sorcery. A liar begins to tell the truth, a thief returns what he stole and gets a job, and a person who brags learns to live humbly before others. In a very interesting scene in Luke's gospel, we see three groups of people responding to John the Baptist's call for repentance. In each case, the people asked the same question, "What shall we do?" John told the crowd to change their everyday behavior: "The man with two tunics should share with him who has none, and the one who has food should do the same." He told the greedy tax collectors, "Don't collect any more than you are required to." And he commanded the Roman soldiers, "Don't extort money and don't accuse people falsely—be content with your pay" (Luke 3:7-14). Repentance always involves a change of heart from selfishness to sorrow, a change in our relationship with God, and a specific change in our behavior.

It's very interesting that all this happened when Paul stayed in a city for two years. This tells me that real, life-changing ministry often takes time. I think of it as "stacking wood for a fire." When I was a boy, my parents took me to every event at our church, from vacation Bible school to weekly prayer meetings. Sometimes, I slept in the back or drew on a piece of paper, but they made sure I was there. Gradually, the truth of God's word and the testimony of sincere believers stacked up wood in my heart. Later, when the fire of God fell on me, there was plenty to burn. I believe that's what happened during those two years in Ephesus. Day after day, Paul taught God's word in the School of Tyrannus. People were so excited about what they were learning that they told everybody they knew about Jesus. When the fire was lit, amazing things happened. The fire came in the form of "extraordinary miracles" (is there any other kind?) and the event of the demon kicking the Jewish magicians' butts. I'm sure that story got around town in a heartbeat!

There are times in our lives when we're stacking firewood. We're faithful day in and day out to speak words of truth to our family and friends and live out that truth in everything we do. We take them to church, pray with them about their needs, and let them watch us trust God in tough times. Each moment of grace and truth is another log on the stack. And some day, God sends his fire, maybe in a miracle to heal, maybe in an act of forgiveness to restore a broken relationship, or maybe to see a hardened heart softened so that she comes to Christ.

Sometimes, we get tired of stacking the wood. As we try to model a life of faith in front of our children, our spouse, our parents, our friends, our neighbors, and people at work, we wonder, "Is it worth it?" Paul told Timothy to "preach the word, in season and out of season" (2 Timothy 4:2). That applies to us, too. We need to stack the wood of grace and truth every day, and we need to remind each other and ourselves that it's well worth it. Someday, God will send the fire.

My brother-in-law Josh Anderson's story of repentance is a wonderful example of God's grace.

When I was thirteen, I walked away from church, and all of its "hypocritical Christians." I wanted to find something "real." By the age of twenty-one, the ravaging effects of sin had rendered me a hollow shadow of a person who longed to return to a place of innocence and naiveté. So many drugs done…so many lives that I had forever altered with acts of sadistic and brutal violence… so many things I had seen and done that a human soul was never meant to internalize. The accumulation of painful experiences had utterly numbed me. I could no longer feel pain, sadness, happiness, or peace. Some nights when I was drunk, I cut my arms down to the muscle, then sewed myself back up with needle and thread out of pure desperation to feel something…anything.

At a moment of mental clarity, the life I had built and all of the things I had trusted came crashing down around me. I had worked my way into the pre-med program at a prestigious university, but I was failing my classes because my drug and alcohol addiction made it difficult to concentrate. The emptiness and dysfunction of my relationship with my girlfriend had finally reached an unbearable peak. The friends, drugs, alcohol, and other anesthetic distractions were no longer keeping the depression and loneliness at bay.

One morning, after having what I'm certain was my sixth, near-death brush that month with a drug and alcohol overdose, I realized that if things continued on the course they were on, one morning I was not going to wake up. Actually, I was not opposed to the idea of ending it all. Over the years I had been stabbed, shot at, and had been in more deadly situations than I could count, but there was something quite unsettling about the idea of death catching me by surprise. I wanted to be the one to "pull the trigger." I made the decision that I would take three days to sober up to get my thoughts clear, and during that time, I would make a decision to continue my life or allow it to come to an end.

For the next three days, locked away in my room, I entered into a blackness of despair. The physical and mental anguish overwhelmed me, and at many points I came close to taking my own life. Then, all at once, a ray of hope broke into my dungeon. It came like a familiar friend, whispering into my ear, "What if God really is real?" I had not consciously rejected God. However, despite the twelve or so years I had spent in church, the thought had never occurred to me that God was someone I could interact with and have an effect on my everyday life. My conception of God was that of a judgmental, implacable, distant father in the sky, who would let us into heaven when we die as long as we followed all of His rules to His satisfaction. It had never dawned on me that I could have an interactive relationship with my Creator.

Like a drowning man grabbing a life preserver, I flipped through my phone numbers and found the number of Misi Perish, a classmate in high school. She was a preacher's daughter I had gotten to know, and who, for the remainder of the years I had known her, attempted to share the gospel with me with infuriating regularity and persistence. Each time she did, I took great pleasure in cussing her out, calling her a hypocrite, and making her cry. However, she was the only Christian I knew, and so I called and ask her if I could come to her father's church the following morning. Despite her apparent shock, she assured me that nothing would make her happier than to meet me there. As I drove to the church the next morning, I prayed, "God, if you really are real, and if you can see me right now, could you please let me know somehow?"

As I made my way to a seat, a middle-aged woman approached me and softly said, "God wants me to let you know that he is real, and that he sees you here today." I thanked her and continued to stagger toward my seat. Then a second person, a man in his sixties, walked up to me, grinning from ear to ear and said, "Son, God pointed you out to me seven years ago when you visited our church with your mother. He told me that day to begin praying for your salvation, and I've prayed for you every day since. I'm so glad to see you here today. God wants you to know that he is real, and that he sees you."

As I sat in the service during worship, I felt what I had craved my entire life, but could never obtain: a palpable peace. I knew that day that God was not only real, but that he loved me, desired me, and wanted me to give my life to him. There was no hesitation or need to think it over. God really did exist, and was interacting with me–nothing in the world held a shred of significance to me in light of this newly discovered fact. I felt I had been resurrected from the grave.

Over the next three months God flooded my life with His grace, and the faith necessary for me to fling myself headlong into this newly discovered reality. I attended worship services, read the Bible, and prayed, the way a starving man eats and drinks at a feast. I began to read passages that told of real life, a supernatural world, that could only be entered into by those who are willing to "lose" the life they have built by their own hands, the world which they had ruled as an illegitimate king. For the people to whom God reveals this opportunity, there is NOTHING they would not gladly cast aside in order to gain this treasure of treasures.

Still surrounded by all of my old temptations and distractions, I began to realize that if I didn't do something drastic, there was a very strong likelihood that I would be gradually sucked back into the land of bondage. I began to pray for God's direction, and soon received a phone call. Scott Wilson, my brother-in-law, called to tell me that he believed God wanted me to move to Cedar Hill, Texas, to live with him and his family so that he could disciple me. Immediately, I went to the registrar's office, withdrew from my classes, and began to pack. Within a matter of days, I was driving to a new city with everything I owned in the trunk of my car. Behind me was everyone and everything that had ever represented comfort, security, and familiarity–"home." What lay before me was the promise of God that, if I was willing to lose my life for his sake, he would give me a new life crafted by his hands.

Over the next couple of years, Scott poured his heart and soul into me. Since that time I've had seasons of victorious Christian living and seasons that were not so victorious or glorious, but God has always encouraged me to press on. I've had my share of dark times, but sitting here nine years later, I still say with Peter, "Lord, to whom would we go? You have the words of eternal life." The victorious Christian life is not one in which a person repents of their sinfulness, comes to Christ, and then lives on in perpetual perfection–having "arrived." It's one of continual and progressive seasons of repentance. With fruitfulness comes pruning, and with pruning comes greater fruitfulness: this is God's promise to us. God will bring the good work he has begun in us to completion, and each day we trust him, God transforms us at a deeper and more profound level. Our task is to trust, hear, and obey, remembering that we are debtors to his mercy and grace. Salvation costs us nothing—it's a free gift of grace for all who are willing to respond to him. Following Jesus every day, on the other hand, requires everything in and from us—and it's well worth it.

Repentance is a normal part of the Christian life. When we experience God's love, we repent with "godly sorrow," the kind that draws us closer to God and motivates us to do the right things next time for the right reasons. It's the way of life for every person who knows, loves, and follows Jesus.

⳨ **Read Acts 19:1-41.**

⳨ **What are some things you can do to "stack wood" in your own life and in the lives of the people you love?**

⳨ **How would you describe the differences between "godly sorrow" and "worldly sorrow"? Which one is more common in your relationship with God? How does it affect you?**

⳨ **Have you ever seen the fire of God ignite a group of people to love him and follow him more? If you have, what happened?**

⳨ **Complete the following prayer: "Lord Jesus, I want repentance to be a normal part of my life because I want to walk as closely with you as possible. Today, I want to…"**

DAY TWENTY-SEVEN
THE LAST WORD

"And now, compelled by the
Spirit, I am going to Jerusalem,
not knowing what will happen to
me there. I only know that in every
city the Holy Spirit warns me that
prison and hardships are facing me.
However, I consider my life worth
nothing to me, if only I may finish
the race and complete the task the
Lord Jesus has given me—the task
of testifying to the gospel of God's
grace"
(Acts 20:22-24).

Paul had spent more time in Ephesus than any other city. He had seen an awakening among magicians, a multitude of miracles, citywide repentance, and a riot when the idol makers got angry at the loss of business. When the riot was over, Paul left the new church and headed west to Macedonia, traveling around that area for several months to preach the word. Then he sailed to the coastal city of Troas.

I love Luke's sense of humor. In the middle of all the serious descriptions of taking the gospel to the whole world, debates and beatings, trials and revivals, he gives us a glimpse of some lighter moments. During the week Paul was in Troas, he gathered the church members together to speak to them. He knew he was leaving the next day, so this was going to be his last shot to encourage them with God's word. Paul preached past noon, through the evening, and well into the night. During Paul's message, there was a young man named Eutychus who was sitting in an upstairs window of the house. As Paul kept talking (and talking and talking), Eutychus fell asleep, and fell from the window to the ground in front of Paul. The people on the scene pronounced him dead. This was not a problem as Luke tells us, "Paul went down, threw himself on the young man and put his arms around him. 'Don't be alarmed,' he said. 'He's alive!' " (Acts 20:10). Paul raised the young man from the dead, and then he had a late dinner with the Christians. (Can you imagine the conversation with Eutychus?) Then, as if they hadn't heard enough, Paul continued to preach to the crowd until daylight. And people sometimes complain that I talk too long!

Paul left Troas and made several brief stops on his way to Jerusalem to celebrate Pentecost. He planned to see the church leaders in Ephesus one more time, but he didn't have time to travel back to the city and still make it to the celebration in Jerusalem. So he asked the leaders in Ephesus to meet him in Miletus. When they arrived, they could tell that his message to them was very serious. He recounted his time with them and the response of the people to turn to Christ, including each of the people who had come to meet him. He told them that he was on his way to Jerusalem, and that the Spirit had told him to expect more hardships and imprisonment.

In a clear and compelling statement of his life's purpose, Paul stated, "I consider my life worth nothing to me, if only I may finish the race and complete the task the Lord Jesus has given me—the task of testifying to the gospel of God's grace" (Acts 20:24). He explained that he would never see them again. This was, he assured them, the last word they'd ever hear from his lips. As a father exhorts his teenagers, Paul warned them, "Keep watch over yourselves and all the flock of which the Holy Spirit has made you overseers. Be shepherds of the church of God, which he bought with his own blood" (Acts 20:28).

Paul then told them something they were not expecting. He said sternly, "I know that after I leave, savage wolves will come in among you and will not spare the flock. Even from your own number men will arise and distort the truth in order to draw away disciples after them. So be on your guard! Remember that for three years I never stopped warning each of you night and day with tears" (Acts 20:29-31). After a few more words of warning and love, they prayed and wept together. They were especially heartbroken because he had told them he'd never see them again.

Could it be true? Is it possible that people who have proven their faithfulness can become enemies? There are pivotal points in people's lives when they need a strong, loving authority figure to step into their lives with a word from the Lord. Teenagers need this kind of word. So do young people embarking on a college career. Couples getting married need to know what they're get-

ting into. And every spiritual leader who is assuming a new and challenging responsibility needs to come to grips with the reality of life. I've known
plenty of people who started well but ended badly—as students, in marriage,
in business, and in the church. If we're not careful, we'll drift along thinking
that every plan will be a success and every person has good intentions. That,
unfortunately, simply isn't the case.

Paul wasn't a sourpuss. He was the most realistic and yet the most hopeful
leader I can imagine. Part of his solemn vow to God was to lead the churches
with integrity and to warn these dear leaders of the potential problems they
would face—and some of the problems would come from within their own
ranks! On the night Jesus ate the last meal with his disciples, he told them,
"One of you will betray me," and each one of them asked, "Is it me?" I think
the leaders of the church in Ephesus probably had the same response when
Paul told them, "Savage wolves will come into your flock, and some of you will
distort the truth and lead people astray."

What are the warnings you and I need to give our family, friends, and
neighbors today? When I look around our community and our church, I need
to warn people against compromises and distractions. We live in an affluent
society, and we can easily think that we deserve even more. When we compare what we have with those who are above us on the economic ladder—
never with those who are below us—we always conclude that we don't have
enough to make us happy. As our hearts are captured by the thirst for more,
we compromise our faith. We give, serve, and love, but not with as much joy
or purity of heart as before. We fill our lives with good things—sports, clothes,
parties with friends, investments, vacations, and all kinds of other things—
but gradually, good things become ultimate things, until eventually we make
them idols in our hearts.

All of us need to be constantly reminded that God is the only ultimate
value in life. There are certainly wolves who teach wrong doctrine to lead
people astray, and we need to watch out for them, but much more, I fear the
creeping and insidious poison of drift and distraction in the lives of those I
love. We need to listen to teachers who challenge us and inspire us to love God
with all our hearts and to sacrifice anything and everything in joyful service
to the One who has proven his love for us.

I love our country and our culture, but I have to be careful to keep all the
wealth and opportunities that are available from stealing my attention and

affections. It's easy to let all the ads convince me that I not only could have that new gadget or go to that fun place, but I deserve to have it and go there! I know I've slipped over the line into entitlement when I think more about stuff than about the Lord, and when I'm envious when someone else has more than I do. The wolves in my life aren't false teachers in the church, but the false promises of more, better, higher, and faster things offered by the world.

The Holy Spirit told Paul that he would send him to Jerusalem, and there he would endure more beatings, arrests, and imprisonment. What is the Spirit's message to you and me? The way of the cross isn't unlimited abundance and pleasure. That's the world's promise, and it always proves to be an empty one in the end. Following Christ promises intimacy, love, and peace beyond our understanding, but he asks us to lay down our selfish ambitions, to let them be crucified so that we can live in genuine joy and usefulness to his kingdom.

Before Jesus was arrested, tried, and executed, he told the disciples over and over again that all this would happen. They didn't want to hear it, and Peter even tried to correct Jesus' thinking. Jesus knew that when those events occurred, the disciples needed to remember that it wasn't a mistake, nor that God had abandoned them, but that suffering was an integral part of glory. In the same way, Paul tells the Ephesian leaders that he's going to suffer, and in fact, they are going to face difficulties, too. They may have been shocked to hear his words, but when they encountered severe problems, they'd remember his warnings and encouragement, and find the courage to keep moving forward.

If we are people of influence—parents, friends, group leaders, teachers, etc.—it's normal, right, and good to speak words of warning and encouragement to the people who listen to us. We don't get a thrill out of communicating these warnings and many times share them with a tear in our eye. But we care enough to speak the truth—a kind and gracious truth as well as hard truth—about the realities of life. We don't have to wait until we aren't going to see people ever again to speak to them in this way. We can do it whenever the Spirit brings us to the intersection of our love for them and their need for a word from God. Paul didn't wait until the Ephesian leaders had been ravaged by the wolves and drifted from the faith. He warned them ahead of time so they'd be prepared, on guard, and ready to respond at the first sign of trouble. We shouldn't wait until our children, friends, or others we love have thrown their lives away to drugs, illicit sex, greed, career climbing, or anything else that competes with God's best for their lives. If we love them, we'll speak words of warning and hope when needed. They need both, and they need us to speak to them with a heart of genuine love.

But remember that Paul's words of warning came after he had modeled a life of faith for two years in Ephesus. He had led these leaders to Christ, and he had been a living example of a deep commitment to Christ in good and bad times. Paul told them, "In everything I did, I showed you that by this kind of hard work we must help the weak, remembering the words the Lord Jesus himself said: "It is more blessed to give than to receive" (Acts 20:35). As we think of speaking out to those we love, our words won't have much meaning—in fact, we'll be considered hypocrites—if we aren't living the faith out in front of them each day. I'm not talking about being perfect. That won't come until this age is past and we're with Jesus. I'm talking about being honest, humble, and courageous to make choices to live for Christ's honor each day in every way. If they don't see us choosing to love the unlovely, forgive the ones who hurt us, and accept people who are difficult to be around, they have every reason to wonder if our faith is real. The normal Christian life is expressed through authenticity in our actions and our words.

My father has been like Paul to me throughout my life. He consistently models a life of compassion for hurting people and a rock solid commitment to Christ. In our relationship, he has loved me enough to speak words of warning and encouragement at crucial times in my life. The Spirit has led him in the timing and the content of his words, and he has been faithful to speak loud and clear to my heart. My life is different today because my dad loved me enough to step into my life and offer messages of correction and hope.

✚ **Read Acts 20:1-38.**

✚ **How do compromises, drifting, and distractions threaten our commitment to Christ and dilute our passion to serve him?**

✚ **Who are the people in your life who loved you enough to give you warnings and encouragement at crucial times? Did you listen? Why or why not?**

✚ **Who are the people who need your strong, kind words at the proper time? Are you obedient to speak to them?**

✚ **Complete the following prayer: "Jesus, I don't want anything or anybody to get in the way of my relationship with you. I want to open my heart to words of warning from you and those who love me. Give me so much love for those around me that I'm willing to speak words of comfort and correction to them at the right time. Today, I want to..."**

DAY TWENTY-EIGHT
THE IMPACT OF A STORY

> "Paul answered, 'I am a Jew, from Tarsus in Cilicia, a citizen of no ordinary city. Please let me speak to the people.' Having received the commander's permission, Paul stood on the steps and motioned to the crowd. When they were all silent, he said to them in Aramaic: 'Brothers and fathers, listen now to my defense.' When they heard him speak to them in Aramaic, they became very quiet' " (Acts 21:39-22:2).

In a heart-rending statement, Luke describes Paul and his group as having to "tear themselves away" from the elders of the church at Ephesus. They set sail for Jerusalem and made several stops on the way. When they arrived at Caesarea, they stayed with Philip, the man who had led the Ethiopian official to Christ. Agabus, who had prophesied that a famine would devastate the Roman world a couple of decades before, came to Philip's house. He had a message from God for Paul: "Coming over to us, he took Paul's belt, tied his own hands and feet with it and said, 'The Holy Spirit says, "In this way the Jews of Jerusalem will bind the owner of this belt and will hand him over to the Gentiles" ' " (Acts 21:11).

The people in the room loved Paul, so they pleaded with him to stay out of Jerusalem. They didn't just offer sterile, passionless advice, they wept in fear for his life. Paul listened, and then he responded, "Why are you weeping and breaking my heart? I am ready not only to be bound, but also to die in Jerusalem for the name of the Lord Jesus" (Acts 21:13). They knew Paul and understood that his commitment to Christ surpassed any promise of comfort or success. He was willing to do anything, including dying, to spread the name of Christ. They stopped begging him to stay, and watched him and his group leave for Jerusalem—and the fulfillment of Agabus' prophecy.

The Christians in Jerusalem were glad to see Paul and thrilled to hear his stories. It had been a long time since he had been in Jerusalem, and God had done incredible things in all the cities Paul had visited so he had plenty of "war stories" to tell (I wonder if he told them about Eutychus). A few days later, Paul was at the temple with one of his Greek friends and some Jews saw them and assumed he was taking the Greek man into the temple, a serious violation of Jewish law and custom. As a result, another riot occurred. The people grabbed Paul and beat him, undoubtedly trying to kill him! The Roman commander instantly gathered some soldiers and ran into the crowd. He arrested Paul and put him in chains as the crowd shouted accusations. In fact, the mob was so threatening that the soldiers had to carry Paul to protect him.

Before being thrown into prison, Paul asked the commander if they could talk. The commander was shocked that Paul spoke fluent Greek having assumed he was an Egyptian terrorist. Paul told him, "I am a Jew, from Tarsus in Cilicia, a citizen of no ordinary city. Please let me speak to the people" (Acts 21:39). The commander agreed, so Paul motioned to the crowd to be quiet, and he told them the story of his changed life. He told them that he had been as passionate for God as they were, and that his zeal had driven him to chase and arrest Christians. But Jesus met him on the road to Damascus, and his life changed forever.

Just like Paul, we need to be ready to share our story of salvation. A good testimony has three parts: what life was like before we trusted Christ, the events around our decision to trust him, and how he has changed our lives since our salvation. We don't have to go into graphic details about the sins we committed before we met the Lord. We only need to say enough to show our need for forgiveness, hope, and love. And when we talk about the moment we received Christ, we don't need to describe the room we were in or what we were wearing. Those details may be interesting to us, but they aren't to the people listening. We need to focus on the condition of our hearts, God's invitation to us, and our heartfelt response. And when we talk about how God has changed our lives, we shouldn't over-promise by telling them that he'll make everything in their lives smooth and easy. That's simply not true. Gospel transformation is dramatic enough without us embellishing it. When I share my story, I tell people I still struggle with guilt, but now I know I'm forgiven. At times I still get anxious and stressed out, but now I can pray and find a peace that I never knew before. Though sometimes I still feel insecure, now I know God loves me and has a wonderful purpose for me. I'm still a work in progress, but I'm God's work in progress.

Over the years, I've learned to look for "raw nerves" in people's lives as I talk to them. Some people feel lonely, so I emphasize my sense of emptiness and loneliness before I found Christ; some are bitter about wounds they've endured, and I tell them how God's forgiveness has changed me; and some lack any sense of purpose in life, so I tell them how God has given me a reason to live. As we craft our stories, we may realize that God still has some work to do to reclaim hidden places in our hearts where we're still harboring resentment or fear. That's completely expected. We're all still in process, and God uses all kinds of experiences, including crafting our testimonies, to get our attention and take us another step down the road of redemption.

Most people deny their pain and mask their fears, but God wants to touch us at our deepest level. Author and counselor Dan Allender has written about the need to go deeper. Exposing our pain—to ourselves and the people we tell about Christ—is a source of spiritual healing. Allender writes, "The answer is simple and often not compelling to the person in pain: because our past, especially our pain, holds the key to our future and to the joy set before us. Our past is a treasure map that, read well, can lead to vast abundance. Sorrow cannot steal our faith or even cause it to be lost; betrayal and loss steal our faith only when we refuse to remember, tell our stories, listen even as we tell them, and explore the meaning that God has woven into every one. If we want to grow in faith we must be open to listening to our own stories, perhaps familiar or forgotten, where we have not mined the rich deposit of God's presence. With better eyes and ears we will sense how God has worked to redeem even the most tragic experiences."

Every tool needs to be sharpened from time to time, and our testimonies are one of the most important tools in our spiritual toolbox. Ask people to listen to your story and give you feedback regarding which parts are unclear, which parts offer genuine hope, and how you can connect with listeners more powerfully. Ask them to tell you how you come across; full of compassion or demanding a response. Our responsibility is to tell it often and tell it well; it's

God's job to close the deal in a person's heart. Like a courtroom scene, the witness shares what she has seen and heard. The conviction comes from a higher authority—in this case, from the Spirit of God.

Derik Facundo is a home group pastor for The Gathering, the young adult ministry at The Oaks. He is committed to Christ and his community, and his friends look to him for guidance and strength. But Derik's choices weren't always in the best interest of others as he writes below:

I first experimented with marijuana when I was only thirteen years old. At that point in my life, I felt like I had two options: continue pursuing my education or live on the streets. I chose the streets which slowly eroded my motivation to do my schoolwork, and as a result my grades suffered. I started skipping school, getting suspended, had to change schools, and finally got expelled. At this point, my Mom made me drop out of high school and get a job. I was fired from my first job at a fast food restaurant because I came in to work high. Marijuana was beginning to consume and destroy my life.

A buddy told me about how much money we could make selling marijuana in Iowa due to the inflation of marijuana prices. We quit our jobs, bought as much weed as we could afford, and bought Greyhound tickets to Des Moines. With the money we made from selling marijuana, we jumped into the dope game.

My first stint in jail was when I was eighteen. I spent three months in the county lockup and was released with time served. This, however, was just the beginning of my legal troubles. Shortly after, I was arrested for possession with intent to deliver marijuana and pled out to a five-year sentence. Six months after I completed parole, I was back in court on drug charges again. This time I went to trial and lost, and I received a fifteen year sentence. After everyone left the courtroom, I hung my head as tears streamed down my face; I was a truly broken individual. It was then that I gave up on doing things my way. I realized that if I continued down this path, my only other options were either a longer penitentiary sentence, or worse, the grave.

I always believed God existed, but I never had a relationship with him, and hitting bottom was my chance to seek him out. I was shipped to a correctional facility where I heard about an intense discipleship program called Interchange Freedom Initiative. I applied for the program and was accepted. While in the program in 2005, I received Jesus Christ as my Lord and Savior and got on fire for God because I was beginning to discover truth for myself in the word of God. Through the appeal process, I was released two and a half years later.

I had written my family a letter telling them that I was saved and how God had changed my life. However, they only knew the "old me," so I knew I'd have to prove it to them when I got home. I left the prison on fire for God, found a home church, and got my Mom to attend with me. Soon she gave her life to Christ and was saved.

During this time, my little brother was on probation for a crime he committed when he was sixteen years old. I was constantly praying for him, but it seemed that God wasn't answering my prayers. He violated his probation for the third time, and it looked like he was going to be sent to prison. As my family and friends at church were all praying for him, I received an opportunity to speak in court on his behalf. I explained to the judge how God had changed my life in a prison cell, and I pled with her to sentence him to a Christian discipleship program instead of sending him to prison. God granted him favor and the judge sentenced him to the Teen/Life Challenge program. I prayed with him, and he gave his life to Christ. The power of what God had done in my life changed my brother's life.

I stayed involved with my home church, The Oaks, and continued to get more involved with the Gathering. Eventually, I stepped up into a leadership position as a home group pastor. Today, I still lead a home group, and God is using me in more ways than I could've ever imagined. God is faithful and is continually opening doors for new opportunities in ministry for me. I'm going on my first international mission trip, and I hope to someday get involved with prison ministry. I've found that no matter where we've been and how broken we are, God still wants to forgive us, heal us, change us, and use us to further his kingdom. God is good.

All of us who know Christ have a powerful, life-changing story—whether we were saved at five or eighty-five, whether we were drug dealers or nice people who realized we were just as lost as a murderer. We don't have to manufacture a story to make it more sensational. Telling a story of forgiveness and hope is radical and wonderful. In every era of the church's history, it's been normal for God's children to tell their story of redemption. It's still normal today.

✠ Read Acts 21:1-22:30.

✠ Describe your sense of lostness and emptiness before you trusted Christ.

✠ What happened at the time you came to faith? What turned the light on for you? How did you respond to that light?

✠ What changes has God made (and is still making) in your life?

✠ Complete the following prayer: "Jesus, thank you for rescuing me! I want to tell my story often and tell it well. Today, lead me to someone to tell. I trust you to…"

DAY TWENTY-NINE
STANDING STRONG

> "Then Agrippa said to Paul, 'You have permission to speak for yourself.' So Paul motioned with his hand and began his defense: 'King Agrippa, I consider myself fortunate to stand before you today as I make my defense against all the accusations of the Jews, and especially so because you are well acquainted with all the Jewish customs and controversies. Therefore, I beg you to listen to me patiently'" (Acts 26:1-3).

If you enjoy movies like *To Kill a Mockingbird* and *A Time to Kill*, and if you enjoy reading the novels of John Grisham, then you'll love the last several chapters of Acts. One commentator said that Luke's story of the early church consists of dramatic narratives and trial transcripts. In these chapters, we see Paul in several different courtrooms, just as we saw Peter and John standing trial earlier in the saga and Paul defending the faith in many of the cities where he traveled. Each time, he pointed people to the truth about the promised Messiah who lived, died, and rose from the dead, and of his own transformation from murderer to missionary. But these aren't just dry court records. Luke gives us the back-story of intrigue and conspiracies with plenty of plot twists.

After the riot in Jerusalem, when the crowd tried to kill Paul for taking a Greek man into the temple (an offense he didn't commit), the Roman commander brought him to the Sanhedrin. This is the same Jewish governing court that had delivered the death sentence to Jesus, arrested Peter and John, and had Stephen executed. Paul, however, wasn't intimidated one bit. He told them, "My brothers, I have fulfilled my duty to God in all good conscience to this day" (Acts 23:1). The high priest ordered a guard to punch Paul for his disrespect. It wasn't a promising beginning to the trial! Paul, though, saw an opening. He exploited the differences between the two dominant parties, the Pharisee and the Sadducees. He reminded them he was a Pharisee, and he believed in the resurrection. This single statement shifted the attention from him and pitted the Pharisees, who believed in the resurrection, against the Sadducees, who did not. The normally dignified body of religious leaders exploded in rage. The Roman commander, who was standing by watching the debacle unfold, thought they were going to tear Paul to pieces, so he ordered his troops to take him to the army barracks for protection.

The Jews in Jerusalem hated Paul. In fact, a group of them formed a conspiracy to kidnap Paul from the soldiers and murder him. Collaborating with the Sanhedrin, more than forty men vowed not to eat or drink until Paul was dead. At that moment, an amazing thing happened. Paul's nephew (the only member of Paul's family mentioned in the New Testament) overheard men talking about their plans, and informed the commander. The Roman officer ordered two hundred soldiers to escort Paul out of Jerusalem to Caesarea, where Felix, the governor, would hear his case.

A few days later, the high priest himself appeared before Felix to state his case against Paul. After his accusations, Felix asked Paul to defend himself. He announced, "They cannot prove to you the charges they are now making against me. However, I admit that I worship the God of our fathers as a follower of the Way, which they call a sect. I believe everything that agrees with the Law and that is written in the Prophets, and I have the same hope in God as these men, that there will be a resurrection of both the righteous and the wicked. So I strive always to keep my conscience clear before God and man" (Acts 24:13-16).

After listening to Paul, Felix didn't announce his decision. He ordered the Roman officer to stand guard over Paul, but to give him freedom to meet with his friends. A few days later, Felix asked Paul to come to the palace to talk with him and his wife Drusilla. Paul wasn't afraid, and he spoke plainly about three crucial aspects of God's work in the lives of mankind: righteousness, self-control, and the judgment to come. Paul's address hit a nerve in Felix's heart. The historian Josephus tells us that Felix had married three queens in succession, one of whom was Drusilla. When Felix heard Paul's message, he became afraid and asked him to leave the room, even though his teaching aroused Felix's curiosity. He asked Paul to talk with him many times, and in fact, he kept him there for two long years. During all this time, he completely misread Paul. He hoped Paul would offer him a bribe to release him, but Felix didn't understand his prisoner.

At the end of two years, Porcius Festus replaced Felix as the governor. Only three days after arriving in Caesarea, Festus went to Jerusalem to meet with the Jewish leaders, who presented their case against Paul. When he arrived back in Caesarea, he convened court and asked Paul if he would be willing to be tried in Jerusalem. Paul answered, "I am now standing before Caesar's court, where I ought to be tried. I have not done any wrong to the Jews, as you yourself know very well. If, however, I am guilty of doing anything deserving death, I do not refuse to die. But if the charges brought against me by these Jews are not true, no one has the right to hand me over to them. I appeal to Caesar!" (Acts 25:10-11)

Festus agreed to refer the case to the highest imperial authority, Caesar, but when King Agrippa arrived a few days later, the King announced that he would like to hear from Paul. Again, Paul explained his faith in Christ and told his story of redemption, which makes perfect sense to anyone who believes the Jewish law and the prophets. But Festus, the host of the proceedings, shouted, "You are out of your mind, Paul! Your great learning is driving you insane!" (Acts 26:24)

Paul calmly replied, "I am not insane, most excellent Festus. What I am saying is true and reasonable. The king is familiar with these things, and I can speak freely to him. I am convinced that none of this has escaped his notice, because it was not done in a corner. King Agrippa, do you believe the prophets? I know you do" (Acts 26:25-27).

King Agrippa may have been amused, or his heart may have been touched. After hearing the exchange between his governor and the prisoner, Agrippa told Paul, "Do you think that in such a short time you can persuade me to be a Christian?"

Paul must have smiled, "Short time or long—I pray God that not only you but all who are listening to me today may become what I am, except for these chains" (Acts 26:28-29).

The King was impressed with Paul and announced that he could have set him free, but since he had appealed to Caesar, to Caesar he will go. Paul wasn't disappointed to hear this news. In a vision a couple of years before when his life was threatened by the plot to murder him, Jesus had appeared to him in the night to tell him, "Take courage! As you have testified about me in Jerusalem, so you must also testify in Rome" (Acts 23:11).

What's the most threatening moment you've had in front of an authority figure? Many of us get weak knees and dry mouths when we're asked to speak in public. One time when I was being interviewed on a national television broadcast, I got so nervous my mouth went completely dry, and I kept trying to get my lips to stop sticking to my teeth. My friends still make fun of me because I looked like I was talking with a mouth full of peanut butter. I've been with men and women who were about to testify in court, and almost universally, they were afraid they'd crater under the pressure. Most of these people were in courts trying them or family members on drug possession or burglary, and some were in divorce court. Paul's testimonies in front of the Sanhedrin, Felix, Festus, and finally Agrippa weren't about being found guilty and paying a fine, probation, or spending a couple of years in prison—for him, it was life and death. But he stood strong because he was supremely confident in the Lord's presence, his purpose, and the power of his testimony. Nothing could shake him. Every time he went to court, he saw it as an opportunity to tell everyone in the room about the grace of Jesus. In effect, his message put them on trial. That's why Felix got scared when Paul told him about God's plan for righteousness, self-control, and judgment. And that's why Festus erupted claiming Paul was insane. But Agrippa understood that everything Paul was saying was absolutely true. If he had been there two years before, he would have freed Paul, but that wasn't God's plan. There were no self-pitying "what ifs" or "if onlys" in Paul's heart when Agrippa announced that he would have been freed if he hadn't appealed to Caesar. Paul knew that going to Rome was exactly God's plan, and the Roman government was going to pay for the boat trip!

We may not be standing in front of the Jewish leaders in Jerusalem or Roman governors or kings, but in a sense, we're on trial every day. People are watching us to see if we'll speak up boldly and lovingly about our Savior, and they insist that our words match our actions. People can spot a phony a mile away. The judges and juries of our life are our parents, our spouse, our kids, our friends, and the people we hang around every day at school or at work. To flip the metaphor, is there enough evidence to convict us of being sold out to Christ? When they watch our lives and hear our words, are they convinced our faith is genuine and our love is authentic? I believe people watch us all the time, but especially when we go through difficult times (they aren't called "trials" for nothing). Those periods of our lives scrape away the superficial masks and expose the reality of faith or doubt in our hearts. Thankfully, they don't demand perfection, just progress and honesty and a heart of hope. We can be honest with people around us about our struggles as long as we cling to our steadfast hope in God's sovereignty, goodness, and mercy.

Let me tell you about a dear friend who put me on trial for a long time to see if my faith in Christ is real. Dewayne and I had become friends after he married Jenni's sister Angie. He didn't grow up with a good church experience, having witnessed a lot of hypocrisy in his mom's church, so he became skeptical of God and church. After we met, however, we developed a genuine friendship. Before long, my role as a pastor didn't raise as many suspicions, so he asked me lots of questions about faith, the Bible, and God's nature and I did my best to answer his questions. For several years, we discussed all kinds of topics, had dinner with each other's families, played golf, and talked about sports—he's an Oklahoma fan, but I forgive him for that. During all this time, he watched me to judge the authenticity of my life and faith.

Dewayne watched as Jenni and I faced the most heart wrenching time of our lives. Jenni was pregnant, and on a regular visit to her doctor, he told her he couldn't hear the baby's heartbeat. He told us to come back the next day for a D&C. We were crushed; we wept and cried out to God, and asked everybody we knew to pray for our baby and us. The next day, the doctor listened again for a heartbeat, and he heard it! Hunter is alive and well today—a special gift from God that we had to lay on the altar like Abraham did with Isaac. Dewayne watched us as we clung to God during those dark hours of hurt and doubt.

Jenni and I often prayed for Dewayne. In fact, I wrote his name on the wall of the church when we were building it, praying and believing God to change his heart. One year later, we opened the new auditorium for our very first service. I looked at the crowd, and there sat Dewayne. At the end of the service, I saw him raise his hand and ask to be included in the prayer of salvation. I'll never forget it. I love that guy. God saved him and began transforming him from the inside out. He joined a men's Bible study so he could grow in his faith, and God gave him a love for kids. Today Dewayne is the elementary principal of Life School in Lancaster.

When we think about it, we're not that different from Paul. God put him in a position to tell people about Jesus and live a life of faithfulness in front of them. He has specifically placed us in families, classes, neighborhoods, and businesses where we're on trial every day. The normal Christian life is to realize that the place God has put us is part of his sovereign plan to take the love of Christ to our Jerusalem, our Judea and Samaria, and to everyone everywhere who will listen. The judges and juries are watching and taking notes. Do they find us credible?

✛ **Read Acts 23-26. (If this is too long, just read chapter 26.)**

✛ **What perspectives, hope, and faith kept Paul strong during all his trials over two years?**

✛ **Does it terrify you or thrill you to realize that you're on trial every day as people watch you? Explain your answer.**

✛ **What do you need to do about your words or your habits to be a better witness in the courtroom of public observation?**

✛ **Complete the following prayer: "Jesus, I want to be more like Paul, and in fact, more like you. I want people to be attracted to you when they watch me. For this to happen, I need you to work in my life. Today, I ask you to..."**

DAY THIRTY
PROTECTION IN THE STORM

"When neither sun nor stars appeared for many days and the storm continued raging, we finally gave up all hope of being saved. After the men had gone a long time without food, Paul stood up before them and said: 'Men, you should have taken my advice not to sail from Crete; then you would have spared yourselves this damage and loss. But now I urge you to keep up your courage, because not one of you will be lost; only the ship will be destroyed'" (Acts 27:20-22).

You'd think God would cut Paul some slack, but his trip from Caesarea to Rome is more like the drama of combining Air Force One and The Perfect Storm. Paul and some other prisoners were handed over to a centurion named Julius, and they boarded a ship out of Caesarea. With Paul were his friends Aristarchus and Luke. The ship went north up the coast to Antioch, across the southern coast of Turkey, and finally to the island of Crete. It was late in the year, and weather conditions often deteriorate at that time, but the pilot decided to push on. Paul warned them that it was a big mistake, but they discounted the advice of a theologian who was a prisoner—not credentials the pilot valued.

A gentle breeze promised smooth sailing, but soon, hurricane winds blew the ship off course and pounded the little vessel. To hold it together, the sailors had to wrap heavy ropes around the hull. They tried to slow down the ship by throwing out the sea anchor, but it didn't work. To keep it afloat, they threw their cargo overboard, and when that proved futile, they began throwing all the ship's tackle, equipment necessary to sail the ship, into the raging sea. Luke says the experienced sailors became so distressed that they all "gave up hope of being saved" (Acts 27:20).

At the height of their despair, an angel appeared to Paul and assured him that the people on the boat would be saved from the storm. That morning, he yelled above the roar of the winds, "I told you this would happen," and then he assured them, "Last night an angel of the God whose I am and whom I serve stood beside me and said, 'Do not be afraid, Paul. You must stand trial before Caesar; and God has graciously given you the lives of all who sail with you.' So keep up your courage, men, for I have faith in God that it will happen just as he told me. Nevertheless, we must run aground on some island" (Acts 27:23-26). At that moment, a prisoner had become the captain of the ship.

After two grueling weeks in the storm, in the dark of night they realized they were approaching land. Paul urged them to eat the last of their supplies, and he gave orders to the sailors and the soldiers to distribute the food to the 276 men onboard. When daylight came, the ship ran aground. To prevent the prisoners from escaping, the soldiers planned to kill them all. The centurion, though, was so impressed with Paul that he stopped them. As the waves broke up the ship, all the men—prisoners, soldiers, and sailors—rode on planks to shore. They had arrived on the island of Malta off the southern coast of Sicily.

The drama, though, wasn't over. As the islanders built a nice fire to warm the exhausted men, Paul helped the others find firewood. As he was bending down to pick up a log, a viper lurched out and bit Paul's hand. He quickly shook it off into the fire. The people on the island assumed Paul was a murderer and the snakebite was heaven's justice. When he didn't die though, they assumed he was a god! (Another example of a fickle opinion.) A leading official on the island invited Paul to spend time at his estate. When the official's father became very ill, Paul prayed for the man, and he was healed. The word spread, and sick people from all over the island came to be healed by the Roman prisoner.

When we examine the life of Paul, we see his dramatic conversion and calling to take the gospel to the whole world, but we certainly don't see smooth sailing. Calling doesn't guarantee calm, and protection isn't the same as prevention. The way of the cross led Jesus to the glory of the resurrection, but first though suffering and death. Paul's life had more twists and turns than an Agatha Christie novel. Even when God's calling is crystal clear, the path is full of rocks, storms, snakes, and villains. When we walk with God and serve him with all our might, it's entirely normal to face severe storms, which God sometimes uses to demonstrate his power over troubles, but always to make us more dependent on him. Troubles aren't aberrations of his will; they're central to his will. When we're enjoying wonderful times, we praise God. When we're confused, we worship him. When we're in prison, we sing hymns of gratitude. When we're in the middle of a hurricane of trouble, we cling to God's goodness and power to bring us through.

Phil is a young man who served God throughout elementary school, junior high, and high school. He attended Bible College to pursue his desire to be a pastor. During that time, Phil's dad battled pancreatic cancer and eventually lost the fight, passing away when Phil was twenty-four. Phil saw his father as a noble man who always cared for his family, but in the spring of 2007, several years after his father's death, he found out that his dad had an affair a few years before. He was shocked, but had no way to talk to his father to resolve his hurt and anger. It was the beginning of, in Phil's words, "a rather insane year." Here's how he described that year.

On May 9, 2007, after I had finished taking my last exam of the year, I returned from dinner with my girlfriend to find a message on my phone from my sister. When I called her back, she told me that my mom had committed suicide.

The loss of my dad at the age of twenty-four was rough, but losing both of my parents by the time I was thirty was devastating. And the way that they had passed away, combined with the information about my dad's affair I discovered a few months earlier, was something that I NEVER thought I would have to deal with. After returning from my mom's memorial service, things didn't get any easier. I was supposed to have a summer job doing my Chaplain training for the Air Force, but something happened with my paperwork, and I couldn't go.

No one was hiring at the time, so I sat around a lot—depressed, confused, and unemployed. At the start of August, I had to go home to get my mom's estate in order. While I was home cleaning out the basement, I received a text from my girlfriend informing me, "It's not going to work out between us." Just like that, without any warning or explanation, she broke up with me. The drive back to Dallas from Wisconsin was the longest fifteen hours of my life. I was beyond frustrated at life, at my parents, at my girlfriend, at God—and at the police officer in Iowa who gave me a speeding ticket. How could all of this happen to me in a five-month period? How did all the people I had come to trust and love vanish from my life so quickly? Depression took hold of my life. If I wasn't at school, my new part-time job, or at church, I was at home staring at the television or crying. I lost interest in everything, and I really don't know how I kept going.

When people have asked me how I made it through, I point to God's grace and my friends from church. I had friends who chose to love me through the hurt and confusion. My friend Paul and his family loved me and walked through it all with me. Andy was there to just listen or let me cry, as great friends do.

Micah 6:8 became my life verse during all this. It says, "What does the Lord require of you o man? But to do justice, love kindness and walk humbly with your God." With all the feelings of injustice and hurt that had come into my life during that year, I realized God wanted me to live in humility, kindness, and justice. I felt like I had been kicked in the gut, but I wanted to be known as a man who loved and followed God.

Going through all of that has really humbled me and caused me to appreciate God's love and strength more than ever. And now, God can use me to comfort others who are going through difficult times. After graduating from seminary, I'm serving as a chaplain at Beale Air Force Base in California, where I'm trying to mentor young airmen and the children of the families stationed here. As I reflect on that difficult time in my life, I realize God is sovereign, good, and wise. As I walk with him, I get healthier, stronger, and grow more in love with him.

God's calling isn't reserved for super Christians or pastors or chaplains like Phil. He has called all of us to love him and serve him with all our hearts. As we devote ourselves to him, we can expect the full range of glory and gore. We'll see him perform miracles to change lives (including our own), but his path takes us through suffering and heartache as well. That's the normal life for everyone who follows Jesus, the Suffering Servant.

✛ **Read Acts 27:1-28:10.**

✛ **What do we need to believe about God, about his calling, and about ourselves to prevent us from quitting when times are tough?**

✛ **Do we always know what God's purposes are in our struggles? Why or why not?**

✛ **How will you respond in the midst of storms if you really believe that God can use them for his glory and your growth?**

✛ **Complete the following prayer: "Jesus, I don't like the storms, but I know they're part of your plan. Help me cling to you through the wind, waves, and darkness. Today, I need you to..."**

DAY THIRTY-ONE | OUR DESTINY

"And so we came to Rome. The brothers there had heard that we were coming, and they traveled as far as the Forum of Appius and the Three Taverns to meet us. At the sight of these men Paul thanked God and was encouraged. When we got to Rome, Paul was allowed to live by himself, with a soldier to guard him" (Acts 28:14-16).

After three months of incredible ministry on Malta, Paul and his followers left the island and reached the port city of Puteoli near Rome and soon reached the capitol of the empire. Shortly after Paul arrived, he asked for a meeting with the Jewish leaders in the city. He explained what had happened, why he was arrested, and began a conversation about Jesus, "the hope of Israel." The leaders arranged a larger gathering so more people could hear Paul's story. Never an advocate for brevity, Paul taught them about Jesus and the kingdom "from morning till evening." As he did in every city's synagogue, he explained how Jesus was the fulfillment of everything they'd ever heard or taught about God. As usual, some believed, but some doubted. Paul reminded them of another prophecy, one that predicted a calloused heart and closed ears. He finished with a statement, "Therefore I want you to know that God's salvation has been sent to the Gentiles, and they will listen!" (Acts 28:28)

For the next two years, Paul stayed in Rome in his own rented apartment and told everybody about the love and power of Christ. There are some indications that he was released after Luke closes his historical record. Paul's letters to the churches suggest he traveled back to Asia Minor, Crete, and Greece, and many scholars believe he traveled to Spain—the end of the earth—to tell them about Jesus. If he was released from this imprisonment, he was probably arrested again during Nero's reign. At that time, he realized he faced impending death while waiting in a cold, damp dungeon, not a comfortable apartment as before. Chained like a common criminal, he wrote Timothy, "For I am already being poured out like a drink offering, and the time has come for my departure. I have fought the good fight, I have finished the race, I have kept the faith. Now there is in store for me the crown of righteousness, which the Lord, the righteous Judge, will award to me on that day—and not only to me, but also to all who have longed for his appearing" (2 Timothy 4:6-8). If the story of these missing years were included in Luke's story, it would have been a much longer book.

Paul had fulfilled his destiny; he had finished the race Christ set before him. Though he had been an implacable enemy of Jesus and his church, Christ had touched and changed him from the inside out. The Lord called him to take the word of Christ to the Gentiles throughout the whole known world. He had many opportunities to bail out on God's plan, but he refused to quit. As we look back on his life, we see a catalog of suffering. When the Corinthians questioned his credentials (even after he had been with them for eighteen months teaching, healing, and building leaders), Paul had to remind them that he had "been in prison more frequently, been flogged more severely, and been exposed to death again and again. Five times I received from the Jews the forty lashes minus one. Three times I was beaten with rods, once I was stoned, three times I was shipwrecked, I spent a night and a day in the open sea, I have been constantly on the move. I have been in danger from rivers, in danger from bandits, in danger from my own countrymen, in danger from Gentiles; in danger in the city, in danger in the country, in danger at sea; and in danger from false brothers. I have labored and toiled and have often gone without sleep; I have known hunger and thirst and have often gone without food; I have been cold and naked. Besides everything else, I face daily the pressure of my concern for all the churches. Who is weak, and I do not feel weak? Who is led into sin, and I do not inwardly burn?" (2 Corinthians 11:23-29)

In spite of all this, Paul never interpreted suffering as a stop sign. He saw trials and tribulations as rocks on the road to glory. God had called him to fulfill a purpose, and nothing was going to stop him. He had a realistic grasp of human nature and spiritual truth. If I'd been Paul and been rejected by the Jews when I went to the synagogues first in every city, I might have thought twice about my strategy, but he didn't waver a bit. Even when he arrived in the capital of the Roman Empire as a prisoner who had been falsely accused by Jews in Jerusalem, he went first to his Jewish kinsmen to tell them that the Messiah had, in fact, already come.

The gifts and the calling of God don't change. We may shift or refine the nuances of how we communicate, but God's supreme purpose for each of us is to honor him, proclaim the life-changing gospel, and help believers grow in their faith. Every act of service, every word of hope, every touch of kindness is a step to make God's kingdom more of a reality "on earth as it is in heaven."

God promises to use every believer in incredible ways and he has equipped them to make a profound difference in the lives of people around them. This is not just a promise for pastors and missionaries, but for all who follow Christ. Peter wrote about all of us when he said, "But you are a chosen people, a royal priesthood, a holy nation, a people belonging to God, that you may declare the praises of him who called you out of darkness into his wonderful light" (1 Peter 2:9). Because of the gospel, we have a new identity. We aren't helpless and hopeless any longer, nor are we aliens, slaves, or enemies of God. We're loved, adopted, forgiven children of the living God, royal priests and ambassadors representing our king to the people we meet each day. Our destiny is grand and glorious, but only if we take up the sword of the Spirit and the shield of faith to fight the good fight. If we remain on the sidelines, we'll miss out on the greatest adventure of our lives. And if we don't stay sharp, we won't be as productive as we can. Sure, we can find dozens of excuses to put other things first in our lives, but none of them truly fulfill us, and they won't put a smile on Jesus' face when we see him in glory.

As I look back at Acts, I realize that God spoke words of direction and hope to Peter, John, Stephen, Paul, Barnabas and other champions of the faith. He speaks to us today largely through his word, so we need to be diligent to study it—the Scriptures are both a love letter and an instruction manual. But God also still speaks to us in specific instances, always in accord with the truth of the Bible. Jackson Synyonga is a pastor who has preached at our church on several occasions. During one of his messages, he spoke a word of prophecy. At the time, I was very worried about a loan that hadn't been finalized for our new building. God told Jackson that he would use our church in a special way. After he preached, he told me, "Many will be saved, and you will touch the nations. Your ministry and the ministry of this house will impact thousands upon thousands. It's who you are. It's in your DNA."

After he spoke and the service was over, I got into our car with Jenni. She asked, "So what do you think about what he said?"

I turned to her and said, "I think it's awesome."

She looked back with that knowing look only a wife can give a husband. She told me, "I think it's more than just awesome, I think it means you can quit stressing yourself and our whole family out over the loan. If we're gonna reach the world, God will surely work out something for the loan." The reassurance of God's calling and our church's destiny gave me a fresh sense of peace.

For Paul, prison, beatings, shipwreck, and other kinds of suffering gave him more opportunities to trust God and touch more lives. When he was in prison, he wrote many of the New Testament letters that mean so much to us. When we live a Spirit-filled, Spirit-empowered, Spirit-led life, we shouldn't be surprised when God works in miraculous ways. We're always amazed by his grace and glory, but we shouldn't be surprised by anything he does. It's normal.

Sometimes, God orchestrates the strangest things to touch a person's heart. That's how God used my friend Monty Hipp. I asked him to tell this story:

> The phone rang at 1:45 am. When I answered, the voice on the other end of the line asked, "Are you Monty Hipp?"
>
> I was still clearing out the cobwebs in my mind, but I said, "Yes. Who is this?"
>
> He said, "It's Curtis. I was your friend in the fifth grade. Do you remember me?"
>
> I mentally scanned all the faces of our class, and finally I remembered. "Yes, I remember you."
>
> He told me, "I called back to our hometown and contacted your brother by calling the Hipp phone numbers in directory assistance. He gave me your number." He paused for a second, and then he said, "I have to ask you something. In the fifth grade you told me that you believed in God and you even said, 'I like God.' Do you remember telling me that?"
>
> I thought hard, but I didn't recall anything like that. I answered honestly, "No, I'm sorry, I don't. But I know that I believed in God, and I liked him when we were in the fifth grade."
>
> Curtis said, "Yeah, I remember you saying that to me. Let me ask you a question. Do you still believe in God and like God?"

I told him, "Yes I do, why are you asking?"

He finally told me the reason for his call. "To be honest, my life is a wreck. My marriage is shot, my kids are gone, and I just lost my job a couple of days ago. I came to the conclusion that life is hopeless. I decided that I'd rather die than live another day. And I have a plan. I have a rope, and in the morning when I wake up, I plan to hang myself."

I could tell Curtis was deadly serious. He then told me, "As I was lying in the bed a few minutes ago, I got this picture of you in my mind repeating over and over again, 'I believe in God, and I like God.' I couldn't get it out of my mind. So I got up, found your number, and called. I just had to ask you that question."

I said, "Curtis, I know that God is more than a statement of belief to me. He's real, and I know him. He changed my life, and he can change yours, too."

I prayed with him that early morning and a life was saved. He revived his marriage, got his family back, and lives in Kentucky today. I learned a great lesson: you never know the power of one sentence of hope said at the right time to the right person. By the power of the Holy Spirit, God can bring a simple statement back into someone's memory just when they need it most. He loves us that much. Don't underestimate the power of an encouraging word. You never know the impact it might have.

When I read Monty's story, I recall that the law of the harvest means that we reap after we sow, as well as what we sow and more than we sow. In Monty's case, his simple, faith-filled words as a child reaped a harvest of a desperate man finding new hope in Christ many years after the words were spoken. We don't always know how God will use what we sow, but we can be confident that the harvest will come someday. Our purpose each day is to be faithful in sowing wisdom, love, kindness, and hope in the life of everyone we meet.

When we see God at work, the glory of a changed life reminds us of his greatness and his glory. We worship him more and love him more. A normal life of love and loyalty to Christ, and seeing him use us in amazing ways to transform people around us, doesn't just happen on Sunday morning in a big building. God wants us to live a normal, Spirit-empowered life every day of the week, at the breakfast table, in the car, when we're talking to friends, during business deals, at the grocery store, in the bedroom, when we're fishing, and in our private times of prayer. If we're in tune with God and we ask him to use us, he'll open our eyes to see opportunities to speak a kind word to a hurting heart, we'll take the initiative to give even more than our 50 hours and $50 to help people, and we'll be glad to tell people about the saving grace we enjoy.

Is that the kind of life you want to live? Don't stop with 50 hours and $50. When we taste and see that God is so good, we'll want to give everything we've got to him. A heart's overflow of affection and glad service is the result of knowing that following him is all that really matters. And when we come to a place where we expect God to consistently break through to lead and use us, our lives will have taken on a new kind of normal.

⊕ **Read Acts 28:11-30.**

⊕ **How would you describe your destiny as a believer? What passages of Scripture that we've looked at in this book illustrate this destiny?**

⊕ **Now that you've finished reading and studying Acts, how has your definition of the "normal Christian life" changed?**

⊕ **What's your next step? How will you keep growing stronger in your love for God, your receptivity to the Spirit, and the effectiveness of your service?**

⊕ **Complete the following prayer: "Lord Jesus, you are so gracious to me. You want me to live a normal life, but your definition of normal is the most challenging and exciting life possible. Lord, help me to…"**

HOW TO USE THIS BOOK IN
CLASSES & GROUPS

This book is designed for individual, small group, and class study. The best way to absorb and apply these principles is for each person to individually study and answer the questions at the end of each chapter, then to discuss them in either a class or group environment.

Each day's questions are designed to promote reflection, application, and discussion. Order enough copies of the book for everyone to have their own. For couples, encourage both to have their own book so they can record their reflections individually.

A recommended schedule for a small group might be:

1. Week 1:
   Introduction to the material. The group leader can tell their own story, share their hopes for the group, and provide books for each person.

- Weeks 2-6
  If people in your group are going to use the book for 31 days in a row, you can lead discussions each week on Days 1-7, 8-14, 15-21, 22-28, and 29-31.

Or...

- Weeks 2-7
  If your group prefers to go through five lessons each week, you can lead discussions on Days 1-5, 6-10, 11-15, 16-20, 21-25, 26-31.

Or...

- Weeks 2-11
  You and your group may want to tackle only three days' lessons to discuss each week. If that's your plan, you may be able to have richer conversations about the ones you discuss each week.

Personalize Each Lesson

Don't feel pressured to cover every question in every lesson in your group discussions! Pick out one or two lessons that had the biggest impact on you, and focus on those, or ask people in the group to share their responses to the lessons that meant the most to them that week.

Make sure you personalize the principles and applications. At least once in each group meeting, add your own story to illustrate a particular point.

Make the Scriptures come alive. Far too often, we read the Bible like it's a phone book, with little or no emotion. Paint a vivid picture for people and provide insights about the context of people's encounters with God. This will help people in your class or group sense the emotions of specific people in each scene.

Focus on Application

The questions at the end of each chapter and your encouragement to be authentic will help your group take big steps to apply the principles they're learning. Share how you are applying the principles in particular chapters each week, and encourage each person to take steps of growth in their own lives.

Three Types of Questions

If you have led groups for a few years, you already understand the importance of using open questions to stimulate discussion. The three types of questions are limiting, leading, and open. Many of the questions at the end of each day's lessons are open questions.

- Limiting questions focus on an obvious answer, such as, "What does Jesus call himself in John 10:11?" These types of questions don't stimulate reflection or discussion. If you want to use questions like this, follow them with thought-provoking open questions.

- Leading questions sometimes require the listener to guess what the leader has in mind, such as, "Why did Jesus use the metaphor of a shepherd in John 10?" (He was probably alluding to a passage in Ezekiel, but most people wouldn't know that.) The teacher who asks a leading question has a definite answer in mind. Instead of asking this question, he should teach the point and perhaps ask an open question about the point he has made.

- Open questions usually don't have right or wrong answers. They stimulate thinking, and are far less threatening because the person answering doesn't risk ridicule for being wrong. These questions often begin with "Why do you think...?" or "What are some reasons that...?" or "How would you have felt in that situation?"

Preparation

As you prepare to teach this material in a group or class, consider these steps:

2. Carefully and thoughtfully read the book. Make notes, highlight key sections, quotes, or stories, and complete the reflection sections at the end of each day's chapter. This will familiarize you with the entire scope of the content.

3. As you prepare for each week's class or group, read the corresponding chapters again and make additional notes.

4. Tailor the amount of content to the time allotted. You won't have time to cover all the questions, so pick the ones that are most pertinent.

5. Add your own stories to personalize the message and add impact.

6. Before and during your preparation, ask God to give you wisdom, clarity, and power. Trust Him to use your group to change people's lives.

7. Most people will get far more out of the group if they read the chapters and complete the reflection each week. Order books before the group or class begins or after the first week.

Scott Wilson has been in full-time pastoral ministry for more than twenty years. He is the Senior Pastor of The Oaks Fellowship located in Dallas, Texas. In the last three years, the church has experienced robust growth, nearly tripling in size—now ministering to nearly three thousand people. The church currently offers four worship experiences every weekend to accommodate the growing crowds.

Scott is the CEO and founder of Scott Wilson Consulting, an organization that exists to come alongside churches and marketplace leaders to enable them to achieve the full potential of what God has called them to do. Pastor Scott has a vision to strengthen and empower God's leaders to fulfill their destiny and dreams.

Scott and his father, Dr. Tom Wilson, lead one of the most innovative public school systems in the State of Texas. Life School currently educates over four thousand students in five locations in the Dallas area. Each year, parents camp out overnight to enroll their children in these schools.

Under Scott's visionary leadership, The Oaks School of Leadership was founded in 1998. This school of ministry is in partnership with the Southwestern Assembly of God University in Waxahachie, Texas, and all students receive up to forty-eight university credit hours over a two-year period and are eligible for grants and loans like any other major university. The primary purpose for The Oaks School of Leadership is to train and equip the best leaders in the Kingdom of God and to be a leadership pipeline for the multi-site ministry of The Oaks and its partners around the world.

Finally, Scott is a loving husband and proud father. Scott and his wife, Jenni, have three boys: Dillon, Hunter, and Dakota. The Wilsons live in the Dallas area.

To find out more about Scott Wilson go to www.scottwilsonleadership.com or follow him on twitter: @scottwilson7

Other books by Scott Wilson

THE NEXT LEVEL
A Message of Hope for Hard Times

From minor inconveniences to the most traumatic events in our lives, God wants to use every painful event to draw us closer to Himself and impart wisdom. In Next Level: A Message of Hope for Hard Times by Scott Wilson, we'll look at people in the Bible and the tests they faced. We will understand that testing precedes promotion. If we understand God's purposes for our times of struggle, we'll trust him instead of getting angry with him, and we'll see each difficulty as a steppingstone to the next level of our spiritual journey. Then, even when we don't fully understand what God is doing, we'll be convinced that he knows, he cares and he'll lead us.

STEERING THROUGH CHAOS
Mapping a Clear Direction in the Midst of Transition and Change

Addressing common transitions like the building of new facilities, changing of staff structure, addition of new services and becoming a multi-site ministry, Steering Through Chaos is the ideal resource for a church staff or leadership team facing the challenges of change now, or the inevitable change to come. Wilson writes from the trenches; his church has tripled in size over the past three years, forcing him to ask the crucial question: How can a church of yesterday transition to a church of tomorrow? As patterns shifted all around him, he learned powerful strategies for steering a church through the process of change and he's passionate about sharing them.

To order these books, go to www.scottwilsonleadership.com

Act Normal Campaign

Act Normal is church-wide campaign, inspired by author Scott Wilson, Pastor of The Oaks Fellowship Church in Dallas Texas.

Act Normal is unique because it creates turning-point moments by causing thoughtful reflection on what really matters according to Gods word. If you're up to the challenge and want to be a part of this community-changing effort, go to www.actnormal.org and register. We want to encourage you throughout this Campaign by sending you inspirational stories of what people are doing to serve their community and its impact. We also want to hear your story... so put the book down right now and go to www.actnormal.org and register.

Luke's history of the early church was a continuation of the ministry of Jesus as the Spirit worked in the lives of those he loved. Today, the Spirit of Jesus continues to live in each of us. In the same way the Father sent Jesus into the world, today he sends us, not just to proclaim the good news of forgiveness and new life, but to be living examples of God's Grace so that people will sit up and take notice. It's the greatest adventure the world has ever known. Are you ready to live a normal Christian life? For more information and special direct to church low resources pricing log on to www.actnormal.org

DVD:

The Act Normal Campaign is designed to a down-to-earth style of sharing Biblical truths will spur on meaningful conversation in small groups. Visit the Free Preview section at www.actnormal.org to view a chapter sample.

These video sessions are designed to kick off each small group gathering. The engaging, informative and practical teachings are designed to be used in conjunction with the small group study guide.

STUDY GUIDE:

The Act Normal Study Guide is a vital personal growth component of the campaign. It combines daily reading and small group studies into one book. The daily readings are short, but connect people to God's Word and give everyone something to think about throughout the day. These readings are designed to be thought-provoking, soul searching and challenging, creating an environment that allows God to speak to areas of life that need re-prioritizing. The small group studies are specifically designed to encourage thoughtful conversation. For ordering information visit us at www.ActNormal.org/resources

CONNECTION TOOLS:

A variety of themed attractive inreach and outreach resources compliment this fully integrated campaign. Each of these low cost resources are specifically designed to communicate the primary messaging of the Act Normal Campaign into community outreach resources. These resources can be customized to your own requirements. To learn more visit our campaign site at www.ActNormal.org/tools

TO ORDER MORE COPIES OF THIS BOOK

To order more copies of this book and for discount information for large orders, go to www.actnormal.org

N. T. Wright, The Last Word, (Harper One: New York, 2005), 50.

www.census.gov/population/www/pop-profile/geomob.html

C. S. Lewis, "The Weight of Glory," a message delivered at the Church of St. Mary the Virgin, Oxford, June 8, 1942, online at www.verber.com/mark/xian/weight-of-glory.pdf

Os Guinness, The Call, (Nashville: Word, 1998), 4.

Henry Nouwen, In the Name of Jesus: Reflections on Christian Leadership, (Crossroad Publishing Company: New York, 1999), 45.

Jack Johnson, "The News," Brushfire Fairytales, Enjoy Records

Video found at www.youtube.com/watch?v=ZhG-tkQ_Q2w

To find out more about the journey my father took to establish Life Charter School, you can purchase his book, A Chance at Life, available at www.nationalcharterschoolconsultants.com

For more information and insight about how God uses pain to deepen our faith read The Next Level. Order information is in the back of this book.

Philip Yancey, Disappointment with God, (Zondervan: Grand Rapids, 1988), 173.

Henri Nouwen, "Adam's Peace," in World Vision Magazine, August-September 1988, 4-7.

Philip Yancey, The Jesus I Never Knew, (Zondervan: Grand Rapids, 1995), 120.

"I Know Who Holds Tomorrow," Words and music by Ira Stanphill.

Dan D. Allender, The Healing Path, (Waterbrook Press: Colorado Springs, 1999), 118.